Married to a "Nice" Guy

Getting Over Narcissistic Abuse

Laura Richards

Married to a "Nice" Guy

Getting Over Narcissistic Abuse

Publisher: Marissa F. Cohen www.PublishWithMarissa.com

Publication Date: June 17, 2024

©2024 by Laura Richards - All Rights Reserved

Printed in USA

ISBN (Print): 9798328416399

Cover Art by: Amanda Sue Potts of Amanda Potts Designs
https://amandapottsdesigns.com/

THE IDEAL GUEST FOR YOUR NEXT PODCAST

Laura Richards

NARCISSISTIC ABUSE RECOVERY EXPERT

PODCASTER • SPEAKER • AUTHOR

http://www.thatswhereimatpodcast.com

As a survivor of narcissistic abuse, Laura comes with 33 years experience on how to identify, heal from, and thrive after emotional and psychological abuse.

Any podcast that wants to educate women on emotional and psychological abuse awareness and recovery, or educating women on healthy boundaries, and learning the difference between red and green flags, should have Laura as a guest on their podcast.

Laura is the host of the Top 10% global podcast That's Where I'm At where she gives women a platform to talk about their dark stories to bring hope and healing to others. She focuses on narcissistic abuse awareness and recovery, and loving yourself through your healing! During her time of healing after her divorce she uncovered the lies that she had lived with being married to a narcissist who was emotionally abusing her. On her journey she has learned to identify the warning signs of emotional abuse, gaslighting, and narcissism, and helps women to understand emotional abuse. She brings hope to others, so that they know they are not alone, and help them see healing is possible.

Listen to Laura here as a podcast guest on the Toxic Love Transformation Podcast

What Others Are Saying About **LAURA RICHARDS** and Her Work with Narcissistic Abuse Recovery

Seeing Laura transform has been such an honor. Knowing how much the work she does will help women who have walked a similar path makes me excited for the ladies that get to meet & work with her. This isn't just a business for her, it's a mission to set women free and love on them with this work. The world needs more women with this much conviction, kindness & heart to serve.

- **Gabi Garland** CEO Resilient Heart
Agency & Resilient Voice Media.
Host of Resilient Heart Podcast

Laura Richards is a fierce survivor and advocate for those suffering from narcissistic abuse. She uses her personal experience and wealth of knowledge to help guide survivors to feel relatable and recognize abusive behaviors and red flags. Learning through her experiences will no doubt help thousands of people identify why they're feeling unhappy, encourage them to leave their abuse, and find true happiness and self-love!

-**Marissa F. Cohen**
National Campus Speaker of the Year
6x Best Selling Author of Breaking Through
the Silence & The Healing From Emotional
Abuse Philosophy
National Survivor of the Year
Host of the Internationally Awarded
Podcast Healing From Emotional Abuse

I've known Laura for over 15 years. I knew her when she was married, and I've seen so much growth in Laura since she divorced. She is doing the work to heal from narcissistic abuse, she started a podcast and now she is helping other women heal from narcissistic abuse. It's been a pleasure watching Laura grow and find herself.

-Angie Bergen, Empowerment
Coach For Women Over 50,
Author,and Course Creator

Laura Richards offers a raw and honest perspective on navigating a narcissistic marriage through her personal journal entries. Her vulnerability and authenticity shine through as she shares the struggles and triumphs of her own experience. I highly recommend this book for anyone seeking to break free from toxic relationships and find empowerment.

-Dawn Renee Bova
Catch Some SoulShine Podcast

Laura is an inspiration to all women! She encourages women to live in truth and to understand and pursue their worth. She champions us to live fearlessly, to explore our deepest desires and live life unapologetically.

-Jamila Merritt

THE IDEAL PROFESSIONAL SPEAKER FOR YOUR NEXT EVENT

Laura Richards

NARCISSISTIC ABUSE RECOVERY EXPERT

PODCASTER • SPEAKER • AUTHOR

http://www.thatswhereimatpodcast.com

As a survivor of narcissistic abuse, Laura comes with 33 years experience on how to identify, heal from, and thrive after emotional and psychological abuse.

Any organization that wants to educate women on emotional and psychological abuse awareness and recovery, or educating women on healthy boundaries, and learning the difference between red and green flags, should hire Laura as a speaker or workshop trainer.

Laura is the host of the Top 10% global podcast That's Where I'm At where she gives women a platform to talk about their dark stories to bring hope and healing to others. She focuses on narcissistic abuse awareness and recovery, and loving yourself through your healing! During her time of healing after her divorce she uncovered the lies that she had lived with being married to a narcissist who was emotionally abusing her. On her journey she has learned to identify the warning signs of emotional abuse, gaslighting, and narcissism, and helps women to understand emotional abuse. She brings hope to others, so that they know they are not alone, and help them see healing is possible.

Dedication

This book is dedicated to all the brave people who said "This fucked up shit will not be my story!" and you packed up all your stuff and left to go find your happily ever after. I see you, I hear you, and I believe you.

I'd also like to dedicate this book to all of the amazing people who have stood by my side as I fell into a pit of despair, and instead of throwing dirt on me, extended their hand to pull me out.

Special acknowledgment goes to the following people:

Gabi, thank you for being my ultimate hype girl, and biggest supporter. Even when all I could do was cry, you were there to listen and tell me I was going to survive. You make me feel like I can take on the world!

Tamatha, I am so thankful you came back into my life at the exact moment I needed you. You've never been anything but an amazing friend and fierce supporter since we were 11 years old. That's why you stood by me when I married him and when I left him. I'm thankful for that!

Angie, Thank you for helping me dream again! You heard the cry of my heart, and helped me heal with your coaching, but also with your friendship! Thank you for helping me take my scrambled ideas and turn them into something so I can help women just like me!

Jamie, my Disney Princess (or perhaps villain)! Thank you for always being there for me and for truly getting me. I'm not sure if you understand how much it means that you get me. You are a beautiful example of what it means to be a real friend. I am thankful for you!

Lauren, Charlie, and Evan, I am so grateful for who you've become as adults. I love you three so much! I do this work, do the healing, and tell this story, so that when they say "it runs in the family" we can say "it runs out here". I want nothing but the best for you! Thank you for encouraging me to choose the best for myself, too!

My group of Friday Coffee Shop Girls, you know who you are. You were there from the beginning to pick up the pieces of my shattered life, and help me create something even more beautiful than I could have ever imagined. Thank you for fighting for me (sometimes even offering to literally), for always praying for me, and for lighting the path to hope when I couldn't see it. I am forever grateful!

Dear Reader,

I am so glad you're here and that you're reading this! I'm so glad, because you've most likely decided to make a change in your life that will serve you for the better.

He's such a nice guy! Have you ever heard that about your person. I wanted to shout from the rooftops, "But you should hear how he talks to me at home!", "You should see how he treats me at home!" But that's the point, isn't it? No one else will see it. They don't abuse everyone. They usually only have one target.

When my friends would meet him they would always have rave reviews about what a "nice guy" my ex was. Everyone loved him! He went out of his way to help others. He would drop everything to help the world, while leaving his wife at home sad, confused, and alone.

He would announce during our fights how much everyone else in this world likes him, but I have so many problems with him! His yelling and protesting was just so that I wouldn't hold him accountable for his behavior. His proclamations of "Everyone else thinks I'm great!" made me feel like I was missing something. Maybe I was too critical like he said I was. I learned how to be quiet, and let him do whatever he wanted if it meant keeping the peace.

I felt so confused. He wasn't so great at home. He acted like a toddler not getting his way. He wanted what he wanted, and if he didn't get it, well, then there would be problems. Ridicule and stonewalling were always on tap. He would ignore me to make me apologize, and get in line.

This book is a true experience that I've had about my 33 year relationship and marriage to a covert narcissist. I wanted to tell you my story, because I believe what happened to me could help you not make the same mistakes I did. I also hope it helps you to feel less alone if you are going through or have gone through abuse. Even if you've already been in an abusive relationship and now you're healing from it, I know that my book will be helpful and encouraging to you!

As I've been healing from narcissistic abuse I've gotten more and more clarity. When you're in the middle of it, you're often foggy headed from the gaslighting and lies. As I've been healing I've had even more epiphanies about my experiences. I would be writing a chapter, and have to use my healing tools to get through the triggers. It's amazing what you unravel once you leave abuse. It's so glorious on the other side! I liken it to standing at the top of a mountain. The climb was hard, but it has been worth it. The view from up here is amazing, the air is clean, and the future I see is clear. There is no more garbage to sift through!

I post on social media talking about healing from narcissistic abuse, and as I post on social media, I often want to show the world how I looked and felt before I left him. I want to show you not just my "after", but my "before". As I looked for pictures of myself towards the end of my marriage, I only found "good" ones. I was so good at curating the façade that I couldn't find any pictures of me where I looked sad and depressed. I had become the master of telling a story online of the happy couple and their happy life. Happy happy happy! All the while I was slowly dying inside. It's so interesting that both of those things were happening at the same time.

There are so many definitions and terms in the narcissistic abuse world, so I have included a glossary in the back of the book that includes many of the clinical words I used in my story. I wanted to share my journals with you, and I wanted to tell my story like you were sitting across from me at coffee, but the clinical definitions are important, too. I just didn't want them in the middle of my story. The glossary is not exhaustive, but I believe it will help you in your understanding of what emotional abuse is.

The story you will read is from the perspective of my healing journey written in my journals. I've been keeping journals for years. As I read them I am astounded at the things I see now that I didn't see then. I wasn't meant to see it then, I was meant to see it when I saw it. Just like you. You saw it when you saw it, and we don't have to "shoulda coulda woulda" ourselves and beat ourselves up for our choices or how we're healing.

The journals start 9 days before we decided to get a divorce, and end at a pivotal point in my healing. I left specific dates on the journal entries because I wanted you to understand what my healing process was like and the time it took me to get from one point to another. I also wanted you to see that healing isn't linear. Some days were good and I felt like I was moving forward, then I felt like I took some steps back. That's ok though! It's all normal and part of the healing journey. Grief is weird that way. It's not linear, so give yourself some grace.

I pray that my story encourages you to go on your own healing journey! The road is rough sometimes, but it is amazing on the other side! I know you can do it!

If you want to connect with me and hear more stories of women who have made it to the other side, come check out my podcast, That's Where I'm At Podcast, on all the podcast and social media platforms.

I'm so proud of you for loving yourself enough to do the healing work! Just you choosing to do this work puts you further ahead than most people! I'm so glad you chose this journey! You won't regret it!

Cheers to your future! Love always,

Laura

Contents

Foreword

*H*ello, I'm Coach Rocky Martinez, also known as Rocky Mar. As a dynamic, Transformational, Empowering Business Coach, Motivational Speaker, Author, and Facilitator, I have dedicated my life to helping individuals achieve profound personal and professional transformations. My journey has taken me through diverse fields, from a Certified Transformational Coach to a Business start-up marketing expert, and through my work, I offer transformative tools for emotional resilience and positive mindset shifts that empower individuals to follow their dreams to **create** a life they love.

My passion lies in guiding individuals toward their highest potential, helping them find clarity, strength, and purpose. I've had the privilege of contributing to two international bestsellers and creating the practical advice column "Amiga Mia." Through my journey, I've authored over 35 articles for the award-winning magazine Vida Las Vegas, and I was the Creative Director of the same magazine in 2019. Additionally, I've delivered over 1000 presentations and consultations.

It is my great honor to introduce you to "Married to a Nice Guy," a powerful and transformative book by my dear friend Laura Richards. Laura is not only an insightful author but also a passionate podcast host and motivational speaker. Her work, both in this book and through her podcast "That's Where I'm At," serves as a beacon of hope and empowerment for countless women who have found themselves ensnared in the web of a narcissistic relationship.

Laura's journey is one of courage and resilience. Through her own experiences and those of the remarkable women she interviews in her podcast, Laura shines a light on the often hidden and insidious nature of toxic relationships. Her podcast has become a sanctuary for women seeking understanding, validation, and the strength to reclaim their voices.

In "Married to a Nice Guy," Laura delves deep into the dynamics of a toxic relationship and, furthermore, a narcissistic abuse, unraveling the complexities and subtleties that make it so difficult to recognize and leave the relationship. She shares personal stories and practical insights, offering a roadmap to recovery and self-empowerment. This book is a testament to her unwavering commitment to helping women break free from the chains of silence and step into their power. Reminding everyone to say to themselves, "My voice matters."

As a coach dedicated to guiding individuals toward profound personal and professional transformations, I have witnessed firsthand the incredible impact of Laura's work. Her authenticity, compassion, and unyielding determination inspire me daily. She has created a safe space for women to share their stories, heal, and rebuild their lives.

To the readers of this book, if you find yourself in a difficult situation, know that you are not alone. There is hope, and there is a way out. Never give up on yourself. The strength and courage within you are more powerful than you realize. Allow Laura's words to guide you toward healing and empowerment.

"Married to a Nice Guy" is more than a narrative; it is a call to action. Laura encourages us all to listen, support, and believe in the strength of those who have been silenced for too long. Her message is clear: no one should endure abuse, and everyone has the right to live a life filled with respect, love, and dignity.

I am confident that this book will resonate deeply with readers, offering them the tools and encouragement needed to find their voices and embrace their worth. Laura Richards' dedication to this cause is truly inspiring, and her work is a vital contribution to the fight against narcissistic abuse.

With heartfelt admiration and support,

Rocky Martinez

Success Empowering Coach & Motivational Speaker, https://coachrockymar.com/

Author, "Color Your Dreams: Paid to Do What You Love"

International Best-Selling Author. "Co-Parenting in Harmony: The Art of Putting Your Child's Soul First" and "Co-Parenting in Harmony: Creating a Ripple Effect"

Introduction

*I*f you are reading this book then you are probably in the same situation I was in for 33 years or you've already left your narcissist. I want to tell you two things: Congratulations and I'm sorry. I'm sorry you are at the point of having to even make the decision to leave a relationship you're in, but congratulations for choosing better for yourself! By now you're seeing the red flags, and you've probably decided you can't live one more day like this. I felt that, too. I saw so many for so many years, but I actually didn't really know they were red flags. I just thought my husband was difficult and stubborn. Well, he was definitely those things, but throw in being a narcissist, and you have a recipe for disaster. My ex was never diagnosed as being a narcissist, but, as I've learned over the last few years, he has many of the tendencies of a narcissist.

Narcissists are like toddlers trapped in an adult body. They will throw a fit to get their way, and you better not stand in their way. According to helpguide.org they define a narcissist as: narcissistic personality disorder involves a pattern of self-centered, arrogant thinking and behavior, a lack of empathy and consideration for other people, and an excessive need for admiration. Others often describe people with NPD as cocky, manipulative, selfish, patronizing, and demanding. This way of thinking and behaving surfaces in every area of the narcissist's life: from work and friendships to family and love relationships.

There are different types of narcissists, but my ex is a covert narcissist. According to verywellmind.com, a covert narcissist is someone who craves admiration and importance, lacking empathy toward others but may act in a different way than an overt narcissist. They may exhibit symptoms of narcissistic personality disorder (NPD) but often hide the more obvious signs of the condition. While it can be more difficult to recognize, covert narcissism can be just as destructive as more overt narcissistic behaviors.

While not everyone you meet is diagnosed with narcissistic personality disorder, they may exhibit the traits of a narcissist. Being diagnosed with narcissistic personality disorder (or NPD) involves them going to a trained therapist, and frankly, many of them will not go anywhere near a trained professional to get diagnosed with anything. I went to marriage counseling with my ex-husband and was told that "he was handsome and what did I have to complain about". That was detrimental to my mental health, but I have since healed from that.

There are many warning signs of a narcissist, but it's so incremental sometimes you just don't see it. On my podcast, many people have compared living with narcissistic abuse by using the analogy of the boiling frog. The boiling frog is an apologue describing a frog being slowly boiled alive. The premise is that if a frog is put suddenly into boiling water, it will jump out, but if the frog is put in tepid water which is then brought to a boil slowly, it will not perceive the danger and will be cooked to death. The story is often used as a metaphor for the inability or unwillingness of people to react to or be aware of sinister threats that arise gradually rather than suddenly. This is definitely the feeling you have when, one day, you suddenly wake up in a pot of boiling water living with a narcissist. Once you see it, you can no longer unsee it.

It took me 30 years to see it, but I finally saw it. I'm here to share my story with you so that, hopefully, you will see it, too. I hope and pray you get out sooner than I did!

I spent 32 years as a devoted wife, never thinking I was good enough. I tried everything I could to make sure I was the best I could be. I spent countless hours praying, going to marriage classes, reading marriage books, in therapy, crying, begging, watching videos, listening to podcasts, and in marriage counseling to figure out why I just couldn't make my marriage work. I wanted to be the best mom and wife I could be, but I was frustrated, sad, controlling, and depressed.

I had spent my whole life just wanting to be a wife and mother. Having had the example of a long and seemingly happy marriage by my parents, I aspired to have the same. Growing up, I often felt the need to be loved, listened to, and cared for. Boyfriends were often serious business for me. I was devoted and fell in love quickly, wanting to give them the same love I craved for myself from them. I felt that if they loved me, then the deep wound of needing to be seen, heard, and cared for would be filled! We know that's not how love works, is it?

When I met my ex-husband in college, he was charismatic, attentive, and funny! So many good qualities of the kind of man I would want as my boyfriend or husband! I know now that I was always looking at my boyfriends as husband potential, and not just as someone I could have fun with at the moment. At the time, my ex-husband and I were just friends, at first. We hung out with his college girlfriend and my college boyfriend. The four of us were together until we both had breakups and saw potential in each other. Even though I had been with my previous fiancé for 5 years, I barely gave myself time to grieve the relationship. I jumped at the chance to be loved by someone else. My heart wound was still needing to be filled, after all!

I see now how my ex preyed on that innocent girl who just wanted to be loved, who was insecure, and who paid him lots of attention. I also know now that his insecurities played a part in choosing me as well.

We started dating and had ups and downs immediately. We were together but breaking up often. I was out of integrity with myself, often succumbing to his every demand so that he wouldn't stop being my boyfriend and I wouldn't have to feel the ache of feeling unloved. Eventually, we got engaged, and had a whirlwind trip to the altar, marrying only 4 months from the time we got engaged. Because of what I now know of him and his behavior patterns, I believe he is a narcissist. Narcissists will often have you in a whirlwind and fairy tale romance. The rush to the altar is a way for them to lock you down before the "mask" of narcissism starts to slip. In the early stages of a relationship they love bomb you with words and gifts, sweeping you off your feet, and making you feel like you're the best thing that's ever happened to them. In fact, they will tell you that you are, and that they've never met anyone like you. All other women before you never understood them or loved them like they needed to be loved, but you're different. With a rush to the altar it solidifies the relationship before they decide to change their behavior. They can only keep the mask on for so long before their true colors start to show. Our rapid engagement led to marriage, a decision now clear to me as the beginning of a cycle of abuse, marked by his narcissistic traits and manipulative behavior. The love bombing and future faking was strong with this one! He saw my desperate need to be loved and took advantage. Add in his need to please his parents by doing all the "right" things by graduating college and getting married, this was a recipe for disaster.

While married to my ex-husband for 32 years, I experienced psychological and emotional abuse. I never knew what emotional abuse even was, because I thought if your spouse wasn't hitting you then you weren't in an abusive marriage. I didn't even realize I was being abused until after the blindfold came off, and I started to set boundaries with him and see him for who he truly is. I spent a lot of years sad, depressed, lacking support and encouragement from him, and being told daily that I was not measuring up to what a good wife and mother was. He told me what I should do to be better, and I tried to do them all, but the goalpost would get moved near the end of my attempts. Narcissists often keep the goalpost moving to keep you trying to earn their love. They want you to keep trying harder and harder to "be better" all while they're making up these ridiculous expectations that you have to meet! Doing this often comes with breadcrumbs. Breadcrumbing is when you are giving little bits of encouragement and support along the way that make you think things are getting better. This keeps you strung along, and almost makes you forget the bad times, because you see the potential in the good that is happening.

Even if I accomplished these goals to perfection he would say it wasn't enough or it was too little too late. There were often unmet and unexpressed expectations from him. I felt like a failure for the length of my marriage, and by the end, I wanted to check into a mental health facility or no longer be alive.

But the bad times did not come without the good. That's how the trauma bond happens. The bond is formed in situations where there is a repeated cycle of abuse and intermittent reinforcement. In public his mask was on tight, so as to keep up appearances. The façade was that we were a happily married couple who had fun together, liked similar things, and generally enjoyed each other's company. At home, the mask would come off, and I was reprimanded for not doing things right, for embarrassing him, and for not being "better" in the situation we were just in socially. I know now he was holding a smear campaign behind the scenes to slander my name to make himself look better. It's all part of the game that the narcissist plays to get others to feel sorry for them for being in this "terrible" marriage. I would be at the same social activity thinking things were great, but just on the other side of the room he was dragging my name through the mud.

The other point of contention in our marriage was his need for the attention of other women. With what I believe is a deep mother wound, he would often befriend women from all parts of his life to help fill that wound. This was a constant source of discord in our marriage. We attended marriage counseling about this topic more than once. Each time we came out of counseling with him understanding how I was feeling, him saying that if I would just give him more sex any time he wanted it he wouldn't have a need to find friends that were women, and then talking out the other side of his mouth saying that they were just friends and not love interests. He promised nothing was going on with any of them, but my gut told me otherwise. I watched him groom his current wife right in front of my eyes. I allowed it because I was gaslighted and manipulated, and because I felt like I was controlling and a complainer. Allowing my boundaries to be crossed repeatedly is how I sent the message that he could continue with his behavior. All he was doing was pushing his bad behavior to the limit, and I allowed it every time. Until one day I didn't.

My divorce felt like the beginning of a whole new life. I had waited for years to finally feel alive and well. The day I told my ex I wanted a divorce I felt a huge weight lift off my shoulders. I remember one day he started to tell me a story about the neighbor buying a new car, and I held up my hand and told him "Let me stop you right there. I don't care about Joe's new car." I stood up and walked away. He angrily yelled "What the hell is wrong with you!" as I walked across the room. I felt liberated! I had been trying for years to listen to his stories with undivided attention in hopes that once in a while he would listen to and care about my stories. He did not.

As a devoted wife and mother, I led my home by example, all the while slowly dying inside from lack of support and care. I spent many days yelling at my kids from frustration that I didn't have any help, and no one telling me I was doing a good job, and many nights crying from lack of affection and sheer exhaustion of having 3 kids 5 years old and under. Our youngest son had special needs, so add that to my level of sadness and frustration.

When we divorced I immediately threw myself into intensive healing. I continued with talk therapy, started regularly seeking God for guidance, tried holistic therapy, meditation, hypnosis, taking a vacation to the beach, journaling, and everything else I could think of that would heal my broken heart. That was often my prayer in my journal. All I ever wanted was for God to heal my broken heart. I felt like I spent my marriage with a broken heart. One of the groups that I joined was a divorce group in a church. We worked through a workbook, had group discussions about our divorces, and tried to heal the best we could. some of us weren't divorced yet, and some of us had been divorced for a couple of years. I was somewhere in the middle. I was healing, so happy to be done with him, yet still navigating the trauma bond.

No one tells you about the trauma bond and the cognitive dissonance that happens. How your brain holds on to love and hate all in the same breath, and how learning about his "new" girlfriend would make me feel. Learning about his "new" girlfriend made me want to die. While I saw it happening in front of my eyes, I went into a tailspin of emotion when I heard about their relationship, and realized that I understood why some women snap.

On my healing journey, I found that many people were in a hurry for me to forgive him and move on. Why was I talking about it so much, others wondered. After 33 years with this man, I had never felt this level of betrayal. My heart and my head didn't understand and I could barely handle what was happening to me.

I believe I will be healing for a while because 33 years of trauma is not erased overnight, or ever. But we can move forward in victory if we have the tools and the know-how to live our best life. As I dug deep into the depths of my soul, the pain I felt was almost unbearable. I have never felt so alone in my whole life. I felt like a fool for not seeing what was happening, and for seeing what I did and allowing it. As I spoke to other women about the betrayal or abuse they had endured, I no longer felt alone.

I shared my story publicly on social media, no longer censoring myself. In the past, I would often censor my stories to protect the image of a happy family and an even happier marriage. Many friends were wildly surprised that we were getting divorced. I had curated our life so that no one would know how miserable I was, and how disappointed he always seemed to be in me. The more I shared my stories with others, the more I found my tribe. Women I hadn't heard from in years came out of the woodwork to share their past traumas with me. Slowly but surely the sun came out again in my life. I kept sharing my story, hesitantly at first, then with more boldness. I found those who wanted to hear my story, and those who wanted me to let it go and just forgive. But in my heart, I knew that if I didn't share my story, others would live their life quietly dying in their abusive marriage. I needed to make a change.

I decided to shout my story from the rooftops and start a podcast where I would speak to women with stories that they were told to "not talk about". I found women who became coaches, therapists, and ministers and have spent their life helping others heal from their trauma. They took their pain and turned it into purpose.

The key for me was setting boundaries with those around me. I learned that my lack of boundaries had gotten me to the place I was at, and how setting boundaries was the ultimate act of love for myself. I also spent many hours journaling my pain and writing words of love to myself to help me heal. Always healing that broken heart.

I wrote this book to not only share my story with you, but to let you know you are not alone. I've spoken to so many survivors of narcissistic abuse, and I am amazed at how similar all of our stories are. Same song, different singers. I hope that reading my story will help you to know you're not alone, help you heal your broken heart, give you tools on how to move forward, and to serve as a reminder that you are worth living every day of this life with joy and peace!

Rooting for you from here,

Laura

Chapter 1:

Covert Narcissist

2 August 2022:

So many fucking years crying over this motherfucker.
What is wrong with me?

This was it for me. This was about 11 days before we decided to divorce. I was so sad and depressed. I had spent so many years crying over him, and I realized that this was the end for me. I cried all the time, and he ignored me all the time. All I ever did was cry over him. This was no longer a relationship I wanted to be in. People who "love" you don't make you cry all the time. While I was at my wit's end, I still was not brave enough to say I wanted out.

I had faint recollections of a happier time. We used to laugh and do fun things together, but somewhere along the way, we stopped laughing, and everything became a desperate attempt to get back to the way it once was. This is a very typical way of living when you're living with a covert narcissist*. There are moments of good that keep you on the hook, while the rest of the time is sadness, confusion, gaslighting, and lies. The way they keep you on the hook is called breadcrumbing*. I lived off of breadcrumbs for years, thinking that one day, we would get back to the good times when we were happy. I played along, ate the breadcrumbs, and walked on eggshells for 33 years. All the while, I thought that I was the one who was difficult, not him. He had convinced me that our poor marriage was my fault, and if I was only "better," "nicer," "easier going," or "more agreeable" and gave him more sex, and would basically just change myself in every way possible, we could finally be happy. I tried to be and do all of these things to no avail. I always said I was a shapeshifter, making myself into whatever he needed me to be. It was never enough.

This didn't happen overnight. Psychological abuse at the hands of a narcissist does not happen all at once. I was not told all of these things in one fell swoop. I was boiled alive like the frog in the pot.

The metaphor of the boiling frog is that if you place a frog in a pot of boiling water, it jumps out to safety. You put a frog in a pot of cold water and slowly turn up the heat, and it cooks to death. It's a great metaphor to describe psychological and emotional abuse. If we are unaware of problems that develop slowly, we may never recognize there is something to be concerned about until it is too late.

I've also heard narcissistic abuse called Death By A Thousand Cuts. It all happens incrementally, not all at once. They take their time, chipping away at your self-esteem and eventually, your will to live.

By this time, our life was sad and depressing to me. Maybe not to him, though. He was out and about living the life he wanted while ignoring me by not including me. He would make plans and leave me behind or plan day trips and not include me. He had excuses, and by the end, I was so manipulated and exhausted that I didn't ask why he didn't invite me. Asking why in the past only got him upset with me, or he would make up some stupid excuse (lie) that I was supposed to believe. Questioning him would often start a fight, so I stopped questioning him.

Narcissists don't like to be questioned, and they will often gaslight you and use DARVO* to confuse you and make you feel like the problem.

Our fights were a constant cycle of DARVO. I would first have the whole conversation in my head so that I had the perfect words ready to go, but there were never perfect words. He would make every fight about me, and I would often announce, "Oh, we're at the part of the fight where you blame me for everything!" It made me feel sad, and I would often go to bed with bloodshot eyes from crying so hard. I felt crazy because I couldn't figure out how I was the problem for all of our fights. I would vow to him and myself not to complain as much, be happier, smile more, and generally be a better person. I thought I was a pretty good human being. Many of my friends sang my praises. As I walked in the world outside of my home, people enjoyed my company. They told me I was funny, that they valued my gifts and talents, and I generally enjoyed myself in the world. I was confused as to why I couldn't make my husband see me as the person I thought I truly was. Now I know why. I hope that hearing my story and maybe resonating with my story will help you on your healing journey.

I had never heard of DARVO until I started my healing process after my divorce. When I started researching what had happened to me, I finally felt understood and seen!

Eventually, I stopped fighting with him and was a shell of a person, no longer sharing even the good times with him.

When I went back to school at 35 to become a speech therapist so that I could help kids like our son, who has special needs, he barely acknowledged me. When I "retired" after 15 years with the school district, he hardly acknowledged me. Narcissists may not acknowledge your accomplishments because they believe doing so would detract from their accomplishments. They may even be jealous or envious of you and try to sabotage you. They often downplay your accomplishments and may say, "we" got your degree together rather than just "you" because, in their mind, supporting you was just as hard as you earning the degree. I often cried in jealousy as I saw friends whose husbands celebrated their achievements. I had resigned myself to the fact that "he just wasn't good at throwing parties or buying gifts." He had convinced me of that as well. They will often tell you that they don't know "how" or "what" to buy you. Throw in the "you always complain about what I buy you anyway," and I rarely had one of my love languages acknowledged.

Two years before we divorced, we were sitting around the Christmas tree, ready to exchange gifts, when he told me that I didn't deserve Christmas presents that year. I could feel my tears welling up. I never liked to cry in front of him because it would make him feel bad, even though he was the reason I was crying. Yes, this is part of the abuse and a sign of codependency* in me. I ran into the bedroom to grab my counseling notebook. It was a dedicated notebook that I used to write these kinds of statements down so that I wouldn't forget them, and then I could talk about them in therapy. Talking to him was futile. I would often rehearse what I wanted to say to him in my head before I talked to him so that, hopefully, he wouldn't get mad when we talked.

Have you ever felt like this? That is not normal, and it's part of walking on eggshells! I was anxious, nervous, and very quiet, walking on eggshells whenever he was around to ensure he was happy. It was never enough, though.

Weeks later, I brought up what he had said to me at Christmas, and he denied ever saying it. I had spent so many years hearing that he hadn't said it that way or that I remembered it wrong, and I felt like I was going insane. This is a tactic that toxic people, and especially narcissists, like to use because it keeps them from being held accountable for their actions. I fought back and said that I had written it down at that exact moment, and I wasn't remembering it wrong. That's one of the reasons I started keeping a therapy journal. I showed him my notebook, but he didn't care. I was wrong. In his delusional mind, he had never said such a thing. He would also get annoyed that I was always bringing up the past and that I couldn't just be happy in the present.

There are a few things happening here that I want to unpack with you. Narcissists will do this to make you feel insane. This is a common tactic, and they may even say that you should go on medication because you seem not to be doing well mentally. I believed this for a lot of years. While there is nothing wrong with taking the proper medication for your mental health, I highly recommend speaking to a trained professional to make sure that the reason you are feeling the way you are is not just because you are being psychologically abused. I was told I needed to be stronger, more organized, not worry about what he was saying to me, build up my self-esteem, and a host of other things. These were all excuses for him not to be held accountable in any way for how he was treating me. This sent me to therapy for many years, and in therapy, I found my voice and decided that enough was enough. I was worthy of a love that wouldn't make me cry and hate myself every day of my life.

The other thing that is happening here is that this began the worst part of the discard. When you start to find your voice, narcissists are not going to like it. He began the discard a couple of years before we got divorced. This was when the silent treatment started; he ramped up his toxic behavior with a "friend," announced that he was no longer going to have sex with me, and ignored any boundaries I was setting with him. I was not brave enough to leave for many years until, one day, I was.

When I started going to therapy after my sister-in-law passed away, it was to figure out why I was still crying months after she had passed. I had just been through some pretty traumatic life events with the passing of my mom, the world shutting down for the pandemic, leaving my career of 15 years, and my sister-in-law traumatically passing away from the worldwide virus. Understandably, I was still crying and not able to regulate my nervous system well. He often questioned me and asked me why I was still crying months later. I truly thought I had something wrong with me, but I know now that you are allowed to be sad after so many traumatic events, or even just one! His displays of empathy were few and far between. He was annoyed by sadness and said, "Geez, you're always in a trauma." This is very typical behavior of a narcissist. Being injured, sick, or sad does not fit into their narrative, and you are a bother to them.

Having heard that I really shouldn't be crying anymore, I went to therapy to try and "fix" myself. It was in therapy that I learned what typical behavior after grief was and what wasn't. She wasn't the one who told me he was a narcissist, but she was the one who helped me decide what I wanted from my life. A short time later, I was making plans to leave.

The other thing that helped keep me sane was my journaling. I've been journaling since I was a child with a diary. I love writing down my thoughts and prayers and making sense of what is happening in my marriage and life. That was the thing I wrote the most about. He was like a mystery I needed to solve! To this day, I journal, writing down my thoughts, prayers, hopes, and dreams. It helps you reduce your stress, clarify your thoughts, solve problems, and improve your creativity, to name just a few. It's been a lifesaver for me! If you find that your mind is racing, give those thoughts a place to land. Get yourself a pretty journal that makes you happy and a good pen, and let the words flow out of you. Let the writing heal you as you unravel all the pain you are carrying inside you.

Chapter 2:

Smear Campaign

13 August 2022:

We have decided to divorce. I was literally mid-sentence telling him what I needed for the millionth time and I couldn't even finish my sentence. What else do I need to say? How else can I tell you what I need? You have read all you can about how to buy an electric car but you won't listen to how I need emotional support. Sadly I'm all done. We told the kids and they were all understanding. That is the best thing. We have such great kids. Who knows what comes next. We will figure it all out.

I remember this day. While really hard days were yet to come, when I think back on this day, I am so unbelievably proud of myself for being brave enough to say, "Enough is enough," "I'm worth more," and "I'm choosing me!" I remembered that my therapist had said to me, "You have been infinitely clear with him about what you need. He is either unwilling or unable to give you what you want." I knew he was unwilling, and at that moment, I chose the thing I never thought I would...a divorce.

My two oldest kids actually texted me separately and said, "So proud of you." That meant more to me than anything. They knew how hard I had been working to make the marriage work. The kids always know. We think they don't because we believe that we're hiding it, but they see our pain. As they got older, I shared my struggles. That may not have been the healthiest thing to do, but I felt utterly alone and was hoping that someone would see what he was doing and see me in my pain.

I was tying myself into knots while my ex was complaining to the kids about me. I know I did, too, because I was frustrated, but it was eye-opening to know that he was talking about me behind my back to the kids. This is part of the smear campaign* which is one of the tactics of the narcissist. He said he knew I was talking about him, but I didn't know he was also talking about me. He just wanted me to feel like a bad person!

There are a couple of things that I want to point out here. The talking behind your back is called the "smear campaign." It's when narcissists speak poorly of their victims behind their backs to make everyone believe that *they* are the victim. I had caught him in the past talking about me, but he always denied it by using gaslighting to confuse me or used DARVO to make me be the bad guy by saying I was the one who did it more often than he did, so I was really the bad guy in any given scenario. The main tactic of a narcissist is confusion, and I spent many years confused anytime we talked about anything.

There is no winning with a narcissist. If you think you can just get out your PowerPoint presentation and explain it to them, you can't. They will act like they don't understand even the simplest of kindergarten concepts just to drive you crazy. I was often told that I needed to be clearer in my explanations when he was really just spinning my words and confusing me to the point of exhaustion to avoid accountability.

The other thing that is at play in this journal entry is something I did not know about until later as I studied narcissism, and that is the reverse discard*. A reverse discard is a manipulative tactic used by a narcissist to regain control over their partner. The narcissist may also paint the victim as the one abandoning them so they don't have to be accountable.

Before I said I wanted the divorce, he had come into the room to tell me, yet again, that he was leaving to go somewhere without me. He sat down and said, "If this is the way our life is going to be you need to tell me that you're done". In reverse discard, this is how they force your hand to make *you* ask for a divorce so that they can tell the story that they were abandoned, which he did. He told the kids, and I'm sure others, that I had given up on the marriage.

I remember sort of laughing and saying, "Why do I have to tell YOU that I'm done." He said, "You're right, I'm just too big a pussy to do it."

I started to explain one more time how we could make it work and stopped mid-sentence—*literally mid-sentence.* I couldn't go one more minute or waste one more breath on him.

> "Will this always be my life?"

Yes, waste. I thought to myself, **"Will this always be my life?"** I couldn't go on one more day.

In that second, I said, "You know what, I'm done." I then stood up and left the room. He didn't even fight me because he knew we were done. I also believe he didn't fight me because he had someone waiting for him in the wings.

Petty alert: I want to stop and acknowledge that crass sentence that he said to me. Later, when I met up with my ex to talk to him about something, I used those words against him, repeating what he had said to me, and he was mad that I used his own words against him. Narcissists truly don't like even their own words used against them. He was angry and couldn't believe I was talking to him in such a disrespectful tone. That's because they think you will always be under their control! I would have never spoken to him disrespectfully when we were married because I would have feared the consequences. At that moment, I was fearless, and he no longer controlled me.

So now, until the end of time, in black and white, I will forever have his words written out so that the whole world can see the way he used to talk to me and the way all narcissists talk to their victims behind closed doors. I will never back down when telling my story or using the exact words that were said to me.

And, if you think this is petty, feel free to pray for me.

Chapter 3:

Future Faking

October 7th, 2022:

I am so sad. I wanted to travel with my ex. My heart hurts. Why didn't he want me? Why wasn't I good enough? Tomorrow, I will go to Hawaii on my own. I will make my own decisions. I will choose my adventure, but I will be sad without him. Heal my broken heart, Lord. That seems to be my constant prayer. I know one day I will feel better.

One of the things I really wanted to do and that we talked about doing as part of our future was traveling everywhere. Looking back, I wonder if that was future faking* on his part.

I was often stressed about traveling, and I wonder, thinking back, if he made it a miserable experience for me as part of the devaluation, discarding, and gaslighting to show that I was a "nervous traveler," I "made a big deal about nothing," or that I just didn't know "how to relax." All I ever wanted to do was travel and see things, but nothing was ever good enough. The places we went were stressful. We always had to do what he wanted, which was hiking, baseball games, and stuff like that. I also started to enjoy those things, though I didn't want to go on big backpacking trips or things like that. I enjoyed it when we went to beautiful places like the coast of California. We would do easy hikes along the coast without needing any special equipment. That was my speed and all I could handle. It was just the opportunity to see the beautiful sites and be together. If we were doing what he wanted, he was happy, so I was happy. I was very codependent by this time and would do things to make sure he was happy. Even in the beautiful outdoors, I was walking on eggshells.

This is interesting to point out. As part of walking on eggshells*, which is being extremely cautious about one's words or actions, I would often plan things that he wanted to do. This also shows that his manipulation tactics are working because the activities are all planned around things that make him happy and not around my "selfish" needs. Selfish is in quotes to indicate sarcasm. You are never selfish for wanting to choose activities that you would enjoy on your shared vacation. Please remember that.

They don't even have to say a word when their manipulation tactics are working. You will be walking on eggshells and doing what they want you to do, even if they aren't there. He never said what he wanted to do on vacation; I would just know the best way to have a relaxing vacation was to do what he wanted, and we would have a good time.

I became the master of walking on eggshells. It was easy to do because I was trained and wanted him to be happy. I practiced being the best me I could be so that he would love me one day and maybe even like me! Boy, that's heartbreaking to write. The best me was agreeable, smiled, enjoyed life, and didn't "cause fights." These are all things I had been told would help better our marriage, so I tried to do them ad nauseam.

The day I was writing this journal entry, I was getting ready to go to Hawaii with my family the next day. It was a trip my dad had paid for all of us to go on, but, of course, my ex was no longer invited since, by this time, we were divorced. It's funny because when I spoke to him sometime before we were divorced, he said to me, "I guess I'm not invited to Hawaii anymore, huh?" I just looked at him and said, "No, you're not." Thinking back to that interaction, it makes me laugh. He was already with another woman by this time, and I was thinking, "Really, you were going to go to Hawaii with your ex-wife and her family?" As a narcissist, they want what they want. A free trip to Hawaii? I think he would have taken it. I think if I had said, "Yep, you can still go." I think he would have gone. I can't even imagine the conversation he would have had to have with his girlfriend. The delusion is wild.

At that time, we had just gotten divorced from what I thought were irreconcilable differences, and literally, a week later, I was on a plane to Hawaii. It was perfect timing. I was really sad that we weren't going together because I always wanted to travel with him. But the thing that I knew would be great was that I would be able to do what I wanted to do and make the decisions that I wanted to make. Even on that trip, it was hard because I was still very scared of everything. We went on a snorkeling excursion, but I still wouldn't snorkel. I went out on the boat all day, and we had a great time, but I didn't snorkel. I remember being proud that I got to make that decision without someone pressuring me or making me feel less than if I didn't do the same adventurous activities. Adventures were hard because I felt unsafe in many situations with my ex. Saying yes was wrong because he would be upset if I didn't say yes enthusiastically enough. Saying no was wrong because he would be annoyed if I didn't want to do the activity. Nothing was ever right in his eyes. When you're manipulated, making even little decisions becomes a big, arduous task.

I wonder if you've ever felt this way.

He would often put me into situations that felt unsafe. If he knew I was scared of something like snorkeling, for example, it would make me nervous, but I would have gone and tried to snorkel. Even if I had said no, he may have gotten upset with me and planned another trip to go snorkeling with someone else. And by someone else, I often mean a woman. This is the way he would discreetly "punish" me. He would make plans with others and talk about how wonderful that trip was compared to what he had experienced with me. I was punished by him choosing other women or other people, but usually, other women, to do the things that I wouldn't do with him. It was a vicious cycle of making me feel unsafe and making me feel like I couldn't go. If he had asked me if I wanted to go snorkeling and I had paused too long before answering, he would have gotten upset with me. You don't know how to answer when you are manipulated and walking on eggshells. A yes or no answer is no longer just a yes or no answer. A yes or no answer becomes an event of anxiety and inner turmoil.

I remember a couple of years ago when he was planning a trip with a huge group of his high school friends. We had just had a fight about not having enough money for a trip I wanted to go on, but moments later, he told me he was planning this trip with his friends. We often fought about money, but he always found the money to get what he wanted. He had asked me if I wanted to go on the trip with him and his high school friends, and I didn't answer fast enough. He said I didn't seem like I wanted to go, and eventually, he made me feel like I shouldn't go. By the time the trip came together with all of his friends, every single one of their wives went on the trip, but I didn't. He had confused and manipulated me so much that I was the only wife that didn't attend. This definitely helps the victim narrative that they use so that they can tell everyone how terrible their wife is and how unhappy they are in their marriage. That I was the only wife not in attendance was by design.

There is no winning, so it's futile to even try. The only time you will ever be winning is when you're out of a relationship with them.

Chapter 4:

Cognitive Dissonance

October 22nd 2022:

Today I came to the beach all by myself. I always say God lives here. I know God has me but I am grieving. Grieving what my future was to be. Grieving the fact that I didn't have a husband that could love me. All I ever did was want him to love and accept me. I see now that God was always loving and accepting me. I just wanted my ex to love me as well. It's not so crazy to want a husband to love his wife. Lord Heal my heart so that I can, one, stop asking for that, and, two, so I can move forward in my life healed and whole.

*O*ne of the things that was really important to me was to go to the beach because I always joke that God lives at the beach. After I got divorced, I really felt like I wanted to learn and truly know what God thought of me. I had spent so many years having such low self-esteem from trying to win over my ex's love and get him to like me that I thought, "Let me go back to my 'First Love.'" That's how I felt about God. He felt like my First Love. So I went to the beach, and it was the first time I felt really strong and independent. It started when I made a reservation for the Airbnb. I never felt so free as when I was making that decision on my own, and I did not feel bad about it like I often felt when I got something for myself in the past. I got to the Airbnb a little later than I had wanted to, and the sun had already gone down. It was not quite all the way dark, but it made me nervous because I had to do street parking and then walk in an alley behind the Airbnb to get to the door. It just made me nervous all the way around, but I did it. It was a safe neighborhood, but I just felt overwhelmed with doing things that I had never done before like this.

While I remember how stressed I was about doing this, I want you to remember: We can do hard things! We may have never done things like this before, and we may not do them well at first, but we can do them!

> *"God heal my broken heart." I spent so many years with a broken heart.*

The most important thing for me this weekend was that I wanted God to heal my broken heart. I often signed my journal with the words **"God heal my broken heart." I spent so many years with a broken heart.** Thinking back, it really makes me sad to think about how I lived my life with such a broken heart. I just wanted my ex to love me; he just couldn't do it, or maybe he wouldn't.

After abuse, your nervous system is so dysregulated, and the ocean actually has a calming and regulating effect. I knew I loved the beach, but now my body craved it. The next morning, I grabbed a beach chair and sat in the sand for hours. All I did was stare at the ocean and let it regulate my nervous system. I didn't know that's what I was doing, but I could feel myself being more and more calm with each passing minute.

That is the thing that you're going to find when you're leaving abuse. Your nervous system will be significantly dysregulated, and you'll feel anxious. You may have been noticing you have anxiety, depression, things like that, and this all feels normal when you are in the cycle of abuse. When you leave abuse and start to have peace around you, you are going to find that your anxiety and depression will be very noticeable to you and that you'll want to find ways to have more peace in your world. That will mean blocking your ex on all social media platforms, and your phone if you have no reason to have contact with him. Some of you may need to co-parent with a narcissist. I don't have to do that, so I will leave that information to the experts.

While at the beach, I was still healing, just wondering where it all went wrong, and at the same time, being happy that I was done with the mind games I had endured for so many years. I was sad that I didn't have him anymore, even though my life felt very miserable with him.

I hadn't learned the term yet, but what I was feeling here was cognitive dissonance*.

You will feel sadness and maybe even hatred for your ex, and you will miss them terribly all at the same time! Cognitive dissonance is a wild experience, but it is normal. Just be strong, and don't reach out to tell him you miss him. Remind yourself of the terrible things he did to you, like lying, cheating, and manipulating, so you are not tempted to reach out to him.

I had a lot of friends who wanted to go with me on this trip, and it took everything I had not to allow them to go with me. I knew I needed to be alone. I needed to be able to just sit with my own thoughts, journal, listen to music, and just pray about what I had just gone through for the last 33 years. At this time, I didn't know that he had already moved on. I truly thought that we were just divorced over irreconcilable differences. I remember how I felt during this time and how I was healing. I was healing in a way that was gentle to my heart, and I was sad that we were divorced and that we just couldn't make it work. I hadn't found out about his lies and betrayal yet, so when I think back to this time, it was definitely a more peaceful healing process. I feel like I was being protected from all that was happening.

By this time, my kids knew he was seeing someone else, and my ex had introduced them to his "new" girlfriend. I will never NOT use quotation marks around the word new. They want to pretend that they magically got together after we got divorced, but narcissists are always working on their new supply even before they leave the old relationship. They cannot be alone because being alone would mean looking at themselves and reflecting. Since narcissism is rooted in shame, they will do anything to not have to feel that shame. Because I had started to set boundaries with him in the last couple of years of our marriage, he had to find someone new who would not be smart to his gambit.

In their mind, this also helps prove their point that *they* were not the problem in their relationship. They are considered wonderful and a great catch if they are already dating someone. Don't forget that in the smear campaign, they have already told everyone what a terrible marriage they had and how *you* asked for a divorce. While it takes work not to be affected by the smear campaign, it can be done! I truly do not care what he says about me because I know the truth.

Chapter 5:

Trauma Bond

December 20th 2022:

Some days are better than others. I am in so much pain I need to take my thoughts captive because when I think of my ex I'm in pain. Why wouldn't he make it work? I don't want him back but I get sad that he wouldn't try. I just didn't have the tools or skills. I need to keep reminding myself I am worthy of love.

At this time, I was really having a hard time, and I was just learning about the trauma bond* and cognitive dissonance.

I spent months feeling like I didn't want him back, but I was also so sad about him giving up on our marriage. As I'm writing this, I no longer have that sadness, and I want to encourage you that one day, you will be able to think back on your toxic ex, and you will not have the same level of sadness that you may have at the beginning. With cognitive dissonance, you really hold two wildly opposing thoughts. I can hold space and empathy for that little boy who needed his mother's love and wanted to be loved by his mommy. On the other hand, I do not hold space for the grown-ass adult who chose to abuse me instead of getting help. Deep down, they truly do not think they need help, so they will do whatever they need to do to not feel the shame of their past, and that includes abusing others.

In my journal entry, I wrote, "I just didn't have the tools or skills I need" and "to keep reminding myself I am worthy of love."

This really shows me where my mindset was at. If you are in a psychologically abusive relationship, you will think that it's your responsibility to fix things and change things. It's all part of feeling codependent*. We can feel this way if our loved one is struggling with drugs or alcohol as well. I always thought it was my responsibility because he said I was the one who had the issues. When you believe that it's your responsibility, and then you add in the codependent information that I was being fed at an Evangelical Christian Church that also subscribed to this narrative of women needing to pray harder to fix their marriages, I truly thought it was my responsibility. I also didn't understand why my husband just didn't want to love me and make things work. I was really confused by this and heartbroken for many years until one day; I started choosing myself and my mental health. I eventually started to go to therapy, and ironically, that is where I found my voice that gave me the courage to leave.

Chapter 6:

Delayed Realization

December 24th 2022:

Sometimes I feel bad to say I don't miss my ex. I don't miss the way I felt when I was with him. I am learning little by little that I am a capable, smart, skillful person. I have a million talents that he did not think were important but that was just his insecurity. Even my handwriting was too loopy, he said. Imagine wanting to blend into the woodwork so much that even having loopy handwriting is an issue. I am amazing. Don't ever forget it!

*T*his was the first Christmas that I spent without my ex. I spent the day with my two kids who live in town. We cooked the same Christmas breakfast we usually cook, and then exchanged gifts and just caught up on life. The kids had spent the morning with their dad, and it was weird to share time with them. I was kind of sad about that. I was sad that despite trying to make a Merry Christmas for my family every year for 30 years, here we were with the kids having to split time between their parents' homes. Something I never thought they'd have to do. I didn't know they had spent the morning with their dad and his "new" girlfriend that morning. I learned about it later on. The kids told me how uncomfortable it was to split their time between their dad and me but also to navigate this new world with him already having a "new" relationship that I didn't know about.

Me not knowing about their relationship was by design. When we got divorced, I told my ex that I was going to unfriend him and all of his friends on social media because I knew he would end up with "her," and I didn't want to watch him move on with his life. He probably loved that! When photo memories would show up in my feed, I would untag him, but after a while, I decided that the best way to never let him have any of our photo memories was to block him. I highly recommend blocking your ex on all social media and deleting him from your phone if possible. The trauma bond will not want you to do it, but it's just because it wants a dopamine hit. Don't succumb to the pressures of the trauma bond. You *think* you want to see what they're doing on social media or hear from them, but you don't.

Your first year after your divorce and your first holidays after your divorce will feel really weird but in a good way. If you have been in an abusive marriage, then you will have freedom for the first time. I have learned along the way that everything you remember about your past holidays was a lie. The good times you're remembering are a lie.

Do you remember how they acted?

Do you remember all the times they ruined a holiday or your birthday?

Do you remember being angry, frustrated, or neglected on holidays?

Did you know that narcissists and toxic people try to ruin holidays and birthdays when they don't have all the attention on them? I remember that on every birthday and every Christmas, there was an issue. It wasn't a giant issue with yelling and screaming, but it would just be enough that it was unpleasant. I can remember back to certain Christmases yelling and screaming because he had instigated a fight of some sort. There was always some sort of problem. Our birthdays were very close to each other, and I always went on and on about how I liked a fuss. I start celebrating at the first of the month; that's how much I like a fuss around my birthday. I love celebrating my birthday! I love getting presents and being fussed over. He would say that he just didn't know what I wanted or how to give gifts and was just really bad at it. I know now that he was just looking for an excuse for not giving me gifts or for not giving me a very good gift so that I didn't get the attention I wanted. I remember him saying a lot of times that I would just complain about what he gave me anyway. That statement is gaslighting and manipulative to, again, make you think you're the issue. I did not complain about the gifts he gave me except to be over the top with my enthusiasm. Because I was under the impression that he just didn't know how to pick out gifts for me, I was very careful with how I reacted to his gifts. I would never have said that I didn't like the gift, but by design, they may buy you something you don't like or something you don't want, so the conversation turns to having to return it. It's all very toxic, manipulative, and gaslighty. It's all part of the whole toxic package of manipulation. A few days later, it would be his birthday, and I often made a big fuss. The one thing that was really hard to this day is our children would even say that he wasn't good at receiving presents! So ironic. A few days prior, he would make me feel bad if I didn't like his gift to me, but many times, he would receive a gift and then tell us how he didn't need it or want it. It got to the point where it was no fun to even try to buy him gifts! As a person whose love language is words and gifts, I am thinking back now and wondering if he did that on purpose. Did he stop me from using my love language by telling me that he didn't want gifts or that the gifts I chose were not something he would want to keep to make me feel bad? This is what I'm saying about clarity. I'm still unraveling all this stuff, and you will, too! It's not a bad thing. It's just something to think about as you're moving forward.

It was strange to me to be divorced, and then one day realize I had been in abuse for 33 years. Author Eleni Sagredos explained it as Delayed Realization*, and I just love this definition, as it fits what was happening so well. She writes, "Sometimes we don't recognize an abusive relationship when we're in it, and it can take us time to process what happened, get out of the "fog" and begin to connect the dots. This is especially true for covert abuse and narcissistic abuse. That's why NO CONTACT and education is crucial in the healing process for survivors of narcissistic abuse. Because even after a survivor ends the relationship with the abuser, most are still heavily trauma-bonded, so you could not see the situation really clearly, yet. Many survivors of narcissistic abuse experienced a "Delayed Realization", when you could finally see how wrong you had been treated only after you left the abuser for quite a while."

As you're gaining a lot more clarity, you'll just be minding your own business, and then your brain will think of something out of the blue that makes you think, "Well fuck, I think that's why he always said he didn't even care about the gifts because then that would mean I couldn't use my love language." It's wild what happens when your mind starts to rest and heal.

I took this time of clarity to journal my thoughts as they came to me. Write it down to remind yourself how far you've come since the bad days and to help you dream for your future ahead.

Chapter 7:

Coping Skills

December 30th 2022:

Well, I found out today about my ex and the "new" girlfriend. I'm so pissed I want to scream but instead I'm taking the house. He thinks he can just walk around and pay me each month so he can live scot-free! Ha! He's going to be surprised! Nice Laura died today. Petty, mean Laura came alive and she came to play! Watch me!

*T*he first thing I did when I found out about his relationship with her was to send a text to him and her at the same time so they would both know that I knew what they were doing. The text was simple: "One more time for the people in the back. Men and women can't JUST be friends." I saw that he read it immediately.

For years, I had been saying this to anyone who would listen. Men and women can't JUST be friends. I asked my therapist about this when I talked about their relationship in therapy, and she said that men and women can indeed be friends but that their respective spouses/partners must be okay with the friendship. I was never okay with it. I made it clear that I wasn't okay with it. We had fights about his friendships with women over and over and over. It was a never-ending story. He always promised me that I could trust him, so I did. Time and time again.

This is really the day that I say "my blindfold" came off. This is the Delayed Realization I mentioned before. The blindfold actually felt like it was ripped off, and my whole life started downloading before my eyes. Every manipulative tactic, every gaslighting phrase, every lie he had told me finally seemed clear to me. It was amazing how it happened! Our brain is amazing; it can adjust itself through new connections and brain growth with the right therapy. That's why it's so important to do the healing work after you leave an abuser.

It is also why going no contact is so vital in your healing. If you continue to watch your ex on social media or text him, you will not be able to give your brain the time it needs to rest and recover; therefore, it will take longer for you to get to this realization that they have been abusing you and you need to stay away from them.

This was a turning point in my healing journey. I call this my second Day 1. I felt like I was doing really well, and then this bombshell was dropped on me! I really didn't understand what was happening to me! I had done so much healing work, but it all flew out the window when I found out about her. I have come to understand that my coping skills* were just not yet established and strong enough to handle this big of a trauma properly. I truly understood how some women snap. Keep that in mind as you're on your healing journey. Some days are better than others, and this is perfectly normal. Don't make any big decisions on the bad days. When you are feeling rage or soul-crushing sadness, your nervous system is highly dysregulated. Find healthy regulating activities from your toolbox to help you through the hard times.

Some ideas that have helped me:

- Texting friends rather than him
- Journaling
- Walking or other exercise
- Watching funny videos or movies
- Screaming and crying to get the pain out of my body
- Dancing and singing to break-up and female empowerment songs
- Saying the word fuck at the top of my lungs (the explicit version of Down Bad by Taylor Swift is ideal for this)
- Staring at the ocean or watching videos of the ocean waves going in and out

Pat yourself on the back for the times that you fall down, but don't stay down as long as before.

One of the ways I had been coping was by making videos on social media about how I was feeling after my divorce. Deep down, what I was feeling was the most pain I had ever felt in my life. I almost couldn't breathe. Making videos online helped me finally control the narrative in my life. He had controlled the narrative in our life for so many years, and I couldn't take it anymore. I wanted my voice heard. I wanted my side of the story told. It's a natural reaction to want to be heard and understood, especially when you learn about the smear campaign, but the best revenge is living well. Don't look back. There is a reason the windshield is bigger than the rearview mirror. In my initial need to be heard and understood, I started sharing my story publicly on social media. There, I found women who were experiencing or had experienced the same thing. I found resources for healing and ways to help others. Months later, I took my voice global and started talking about my experience on my own podcast that helps women share their stories of surviving and healing from narcissistic abuse.

As I'm telling you all of this, it's important to talk about something that you may hear from people as you start to tell your story to others. Many people might think and even say, "Well, why didn't you just leave?" For years, I had been going to therapy to heal some feelings of codependency I had. When we had brought our son home from college for having drug and alcohol issues, I was told that if I were a better mother, our child would not be having these issues. I always tell our son that his issues sent me to therapy, but it was there that I found my voice and left my marriage for a better life! He often feels bad for that time in our life, but I am thankful that even a dark and twisty path led me to find my voice and find freedom in divorce. You never know what's going to change your life.

The most ironic part of my journey with a covert narcissist is that the narcissist will drive you so insane that you end up going to therapy, and it is in therapy that you often wake up! You will find your voice and value enough to wake up and say enough is enough. There, you will look at your life and say, "Is this how I want to live for another 40 years?" It's what happened to me, and I am thankful for it every day. **Covert narcissists are able to fool those outside the home because they only abuse inside the home. @carolinestrawson**

> *Covert narcissists are able to fool those outside the home because they only abuse inside the home.*
> @carolinestrawson

By the time I started going to therapy, we had been married for 25 years. When you're married to someone for that long, and you have been gaslit and manipulated for much, if not all, of that time, then you don't often feel secure enough to bring up something that could start a fight. When we would come home from social gatherings where she was at, I would often say, "You flirt way too much with her." He would hug me and tell me he was so sorry and didn't realize what he was doing. He would also say, "You know, I've always been a flirty guy. Since high school, all my girlfriends have always said what a flirty guy I am." Sitting here thinking back to that conversation, it just didn't even register to me that it was a red flag because, at this point, if you've been manipulated for 25 years and psychologically abused, it's hard to see them anymore. You hang onto the apologies and the good times and go into self-preservation mode*. In self-preservation mode, you don't want to see the bad, and unfortunately, it looks like you are allowing their behavior to them. Putting my foot down would have meant losing my entire life and marriage. He may have left me for her! How was I going to live without him? Ironically, that's what happened anyway. I was a shell of a person by this time. My self-confidence was eroding away.

Narcissists need a new supply. If they aren't cheating on you in your marriage, they may have someone waiting for them in the wings, or they will have someone immediately after the divorce. This has nothing to do with you! I want you to remember this! When I found out about their relationship, I felt replaced, discarded, embarrassed, and thrown away like trash. I felt so ashamed for letting it go on for so long and for not speaking up sooner. It felt painful!

That's why education is so important. As I researched narcissism, I learned that the narcissists cannot be alone. Google.com AI says, "Narcissists may have trouble being alone because they need external validation to maintain their self-esteem. Being alone can remind them of everything they are, especially everything they aren't. They may despise others for feeling or being a way they never could. They may also avoid introspection, and being alone forces them to look within, and they despise what they find."

> *You are worthy of love. You've always been worthy of love. You were just trying to get love from the wrong person.*

So when you're feeling low, discarded, and unloved, remember all of this. **You are worthy of love. You've always been worthy of love. You were just trying to get love from the wrong person.**

So when people ask you why you didn't just leave, just know that they may have never experienced anything like this and may not understand. It may feel like it's your job to answer questions and help them understand, but it's not. Keep living your life, keep healing yourself, keep moving forward. Your well-lived life will be your answer. The way you heal may not look the way others heal. It is our own journey to explore, and we now have the freedom to do so!

Chapter 8:

Reactive Rage

January 1st 2023:

When I talked to Charlie the other day he said "Mom forgive me for all the years we thought you were such a bad mom. We know and understand now". I am so thankful for my beautiful children and that they're loving me through this all! 2023 is going to be a great year! Thank you Lord for healing me!

*W*ow, what an emotional thing to share with you all! This is a really important thing to talk about. Being able to heal with your children after the dust has settled was so healing and profound to me. It's never too late to have conversations with your kids. Our kids were grown and had previously participated in the gaslighting. For many years, I felt like a bad mom. I remember the first time I said to my ex, "Why won't you tell me I'm a good mom?" and he told me it was because sometimes I got mad at the kids, and so he couldn't say I was a good mom if I wasn't a good mom 100% of the time. This is very unrealistic because, as humans, we are not perfect. Looking back and talking to my grown children, I know I was a good mom. I just had a hard time not being supported. It made me tired, bitter, and angry. I knew that no matter what I did, I would never get that coveted "good mom" title. Even when he wasn't around, and I would make a mistake, I felt like I was a failure. It's part of the way that they make you feel. Even when they are not in the room, you can hear their voice in your head saying, "You're not good enough." Your conscience actually becomes their voice in your head.

The goal of being a "good mom" was Is unattainable. Imagine Lucy pulling that football away from Charlie Brown. She did it every time, but he gave it one more chance every time. Ugh. If I were close, I would get a somewhat kind word, maybe in a mother's day card, but those "breadcrumbs" just kept me strung along, hoping that one day I would get the words I longed to hear. I did, years later, while sitting in therapy, begging for them. They meant nothing by that point; much too little too late. He would say, "You always bring up the past." In an effort to make me stop asking, but that's so they can not be held accountable for their actions. My ex never truly looked at me like I was a good mom, so I learned to acknowledge myself as a good mom.

You must work on loving yourself to keep going in the relationship, but if you continue to love yourself, you will find that you are worth more than you are getting from your toxic partner. That is how I finally woke up and left my ex after 33 years. I knew I was worth more.

I had conversations with the kids about things from the past that had hurt them and things they had done to hurt me. We all had good cries and lots of hugs and apologies. While reactive abuse, or what I've heard called "reactive rage," is a real thing, it's by design. I was so unsupported, sad, and depressed, and all my body could do was to be angry. I thought I was an angry person, but I am not. I'm just no longer being manipulated or gaslit.

As I started healing, I would pay attention to my emotions, and I began to understand that my mind was getting clearer. I was gaining clarity not only from the time I was away from my ex and out of abuse but also because I was intentionally focusing on my healing. If my body felt bad, I would rest and go for walks. When my mind was racing, I exercised, prayed, journaled, and talked to wise friends. Some days, there was wine and cake, but most days, I focused on my healing. I needed to get better. I was desperate for it. I couldn't wait one more day for my new life to begin. I thought that was going to happen back in September, but instead, I felt like I was healing in a whole new way.

His betrayal was not only with another woman, but it was the years of lies and manipulation. That saddened me to my core.

As a devoted wife, I had been faithful to him for 32 years. At least I can think back to my efforts in the marriage and know I have integrity. I spent years working, trying to better our marriage by attending groups at church, learning to be a better wife, praying for him, having others pray, attending marriage conferences, and taking him to marriage counseling occasionally. Nothing really stuck. Sometimes, I would plan activities that would bring us closer together so that we could connect. He would always give up and get mad. I love to dance. One of the things I wish we would have done together is dance. I truly want the next guy I'm with to want to dance with me. I'm putting in my order! I had purchased this dance instruction video and he agreed to attempt it with me. It was a simple couples dance. We weren't going anywhere with it; I just wanted to dance with him in our living room. We got through the first half hour of the lesson before he gave up and said he didn't understand the moves. By the end, I was in the bedroom crying for making him "be something he's not" and "try something you know I hate." He didn't see it as a way to connect; to him, I was simply trying to be controlling.

This is all very typical behavior of someone who is toxic. In healthy relationships, when you are trying to connect with your partner, you will find ways to work it out. Your relationship is improved by the conversation.

When you're in a toxic relationship, the toxic person will just find a way to blame you for what's going on, with no attempt at salvaging the relationship. They just want to be right; they want you to be blamed, and they do not want to be held accountable for their actions. This isn't just for romantic partners. This is found in friendships and families as well. Who is attempting to salvage a relationship or reconcile with you? Look for connection moments and them taking responsibility for their actions. That is how you will find and attract healthy people in your life.

I didn't know that the anger I felt would help propel me forward in my healing. I saw this quote, and I hope it encourages you like it did to me. "Anger is a necessary stage of the healing process. Be willing to feel your anger, even though it may seem endless. The more you truly feel it, the more it will begin to dissipate and the more you will heal." ELISABETH KUBLER-ROSS loveliveson.com

> *"Anger is a necessary stage of the healing process. Be willing to feel your anger, even though it may seem endless. The more you truly feel it, the more it will begin to dissipate and the more you will heal."*
> *ELISABETH KUBLER-ROSS*
> *loveliveson.com*

61

Chapter 9:

Gaslighting

3 january 2023:

I couldn't control myself. I sent my ex a really rude text asking how long they've been sleeping together. I got everything out that I wanted to and I feel better! He actually responded. He denies everything like the narcissist he is. I also spoke to Lauren for about 2 hours laughing and then setting boundaries for when we discuss my ex. She is very hurt by his flippant behavior and how he thinks everyone should just be happy for him. I'm going to continue to heal and grow from this experience. The amount of betrayal sucks, but that's what a narcissist does. He sucked the life out of me for so long and now I'm free! Thank you Lord I'm free! Free to finally be me! Free!

Sending him this text was not something I should have done, but in the early stages of healing, your body is aching for a hit of that dopamine that you get from texting them or peeking at their social media. I felt so out of control at this point, and having had my voice stifled for so many years, I just had to finally get it out of me. Professionals do not recommend that you do this! They highly recommend that you write the text or letter but do not send it to your ex. Finding out about his "new" girlfriend felt like I was starting my healing all over again. I wanted to call him out on all his lies because he had been lying about his relationship with this woman for so long. I wanted to let him know I knew what he was doing. I felt like I had started over on my healing because even though I had coping skills, they were not strong enough to handle this big of a stressor yet. I was in the infancy of my healing, having only been healing from the divorce for three months, and my coping skills were just not strong enough to handle learning about the betrayal. Before I found out about the girlfriend, I truly thought we were divorced because of irreconcilable differences. After I found out about the girlfriend, it felt like the blindfold was ripped off, and I saw him for who he truly was. In my best Bella-from-Twilight voice, I said what he was..."narcissist." Everything started downloading in my brain: every lie, every narcissistic trait! I also started seeing information about narcissistic abuse everywhere. I finally felt understood and I understood what had been happening to me for so many years!

My kids also talked to me once I told them I knew. They told me everything and anything I wanted to know. This only validated what I had thought he was all along. He was a liar and cheater, and the first words out of my mouth when I found out about her were, "I knew I was right!". The amount of clarity you get after leaving abuse is incredible. It takes time, but as you recover your brain will start to put the puzzle pieces together. It was hard to see it before, but I got clarity as my brain rested, and I was no longer being gaslit or manipulated.

You will, too.

I started to voraciously research narcissistic abuse, and I realized that all of these years, I wasn't crazy. That was the biggest vindication. I spent so many years in turmoil, confusion, sadness, depression, and in prayer, hoping and praying our marriage would work. I would hope and pray that he would just understand me, that tomorrow I would just do better, and that he would finally love me. I think back now, and I think, "how fucking sad is that?' I truly thought that if I could be better tomorrow, he would finally love me and show me love. He said he loved me, but that doesn't mean he actually did because I don't think that narcissists actually do know how to love. They know how to go through the motions and love bombs with gifts and words, but do they truly love? I really wanted him to like me as well. I felt like we were just going through the motions. Every once in a while, I felt good, but I would journal, "I wish my husband liked me. I don't think he does." He didn't. They only like and love people who can do something for them. They use others to get their needs met. As hard as that is to hear, it's the truth. Try having any kind of relationship with a narcissist or toxic person, and see what happens when you do not reciprocate or do something for them. You will get dropped because you will no longer be useful.

He denied everything I accused him of. I will admit the text I sent was vile. My anger definitely showed in that moment. The reason I sent a vile text was because I was furious. I've never been so angry in my entire life. It became so clear to me, not just out of jealousy, but because I was still furious at him. I understand two things about her. She's been groomed since the day they met to be his next supply. She was way too flirty in front of me with him, and since I walked on eggshells around him, I didn't stop it like I would today. We had many conversations about her, and he always apologized and told me he wouldn't do it again. But he would always do it again. She was also not the first woman we had issues with. I truly trusted him, but I feel like he pushed the boundaries when it came to flirting and having an emotional affair. It's not easy to just walk out when you are manipulated and gaslit. **It is a sign of past trauma when you try to convince others to treat you better rather than leaving the relationship.** I have done this all of my life. If I could be better, do something better, and convince the other person, maybe they wouldn't leave me. Ugh. That was a hard one to realize. Now that I know that, it makes it easy when friendships end, or toxic people leave my life. I don't chase people the way I used to. **When you've worked on your self-worth, you don't chase people, and you don't beg for love.**

Sending a text felt good at that moment, but that dopamine rush was temporary. It didn't solve any of my problems or give me the relief or the answers I wanted, just like if you look at their social media. You may be curious, but it will hurt, trust me. Go full no contact, and block him everywhere you can.

Don't get me wrong. Sending the text and saying things that I had wanted to say for 33 years felt really good! After 33 years for him to pick up and walk away and get a new toy like a toddler because he was tired of the old one, it felt good to call that out in a text. I don't want you to think it won't feel good, but it is only temporary. Unfortunately, you will "prove him right" that you are the crazy ex. Most likely, that's what he's been telling others. I was okay with being the "crazy ex" in his story because I knew I was acting like one. But I also knew the truth of our entire relationship. He was talking about me behind my back and setting me up anyway.

As hard as this is, you just have to get used to it. We don't want to be talked about, and we may want to defend ourselves, but you don't have to. You know the truth. You can tell your story. There are people who will believe you, and there are people who won't. In secondary gaslighting*, you may hear, "Are you sure that happened to you?" You have to be strong and remember that you know the truth. They are masters at getting others to think they are a nice guy because the abuse is only happening inside the home. Others see them as charming and successful members of society. They do not know who they are inside your home.

Chapter 10:

Fear of Retribution

January 13th 2023:

I don't want him back but my heart hurts. I had a great conversation with Evan today. Lots of healing. I told him how I feel about them dating, he asked so I told him. My next practice is detachment. I'm heartbroken for Lauren and Charlie. They're so disappointed in their dad. I am too. I asked my ex if he would meet me to talk yesterday. We talked for an hour and a half. I just wanted to know why he wouldn't just ask me for a divorce. He had no answer for me. I told him that him dating her is bulllshit They flirted for 7 years and that's why a month later they were together. If I had an issue why wouldn't he stop? He had no answer for me. Lauren talked to him and they fought. She won't be talking to him until he admits what he's done sucks. He won't so she has to live without a dad. I hate him for that, but God has started to redeem the lost years. All the years I sat thinking I was a terrible mother I was actually just gaslit.

his was a really important date because I reached out to my ex to ask him to meet me so that we could talk. My flesh wanted answers, and I thought he would give them to me. In hindsight, this was a terrible idea. We met in a public park, and I asked him why he wasn't truthful with me about her and why he didn't just ask me for a divorce. Again, he had no answer for me and said that they were just friends. He just thought they would always be just friends. I told him that he was lying, that they had flirted for seven years right in front of my face, and if they were truly "just friends," then how did they get together so fast?

The Narcissist will spin their story any way they need it spun so that they can be free of any accountability.

This is what a trauma bond looks like.

I remember that day we talked for an hour and a half, and I was still very much trauma bonded to him. This picture explains the trauma bond perfectly. You are so bonded to your perpetrator that they abuse you, and they also will soothe you. He did this to me for so many years, and it happened again on this day. The day that I met up with him, I was furious with him. I was yelling at him and saying things that I was never brave enough to say to him when we were married. When we were married, I never spoke my mind or said what I truly felt for fear of retribution. I was crying to him about the betrayal and the lies, and I asked him to hug me because I was so sad. Thinking back on that, it is so disturbing that I felt that way. I hated him so much. He was with her; he made me furious, yet I was convinced he was the only one who could soothe me, just like all the years we were together. It was the trauma bond in full effect.

It's so heartbreaking to think about it, but I want you to understand that it's normal, and it happens to the best of us. Even if you've been doing a lot of healing work, it can still happen. Sadly, I am proof of that.

The best way to get over the trauma bond is to go full no contact. No contact means blocked on all social media, and do not have any contact with him unless you have to for, say, your children. If you have to have a relationship with your ex, who is a narcissist; I recommend using the gray rock method* and only responding to their texts using simple one or two words. I do not have to co-parent with him, so I cannot speak on this. I know that there are tons of resources out there to help you, so go searching!

My two oldest always wanted an update, so I called our daughter after talking to their dad. She told me she was going to call him to talk to him. Weeks earlier, he had been near the city she lives in and wanted her to meet his "new" girlfriend. Our daughter refused, saying that she felt it was too soon for him to be dating, especially that particular woman. She called her dad and called him out on some things, and he yelled at her, which he's never done, really. He asked her why she couldn't be happy for him. He just wanted to be happy. Remember, the story that has been told is that his marriage to me was miserable. The story going forward is that everyone has to get on board because he's finally happy. To this day, she feels like he chose his girlfriend over his daughter. From that day, she asked him not to contact her anymore until she was ready. At the writing of this book, she still has not spoken to her dad. He became a different person to the kids when I was not there to be the buffer, and they started to see him for who he truly was. I never thought about how I would protect his image until this happened. I curated our life and protected what people saw so they wouldn't know what was happening behind closed doors. I helped curate the façade while we were married, and our kids saw a different person after the divorce.

One of the things that I saw as a theme in my journals was that I wanted to understand. You may be feeling this way as well. I wanted him to explain to me why he hurt me, but the thing you need to understand is that the person who hurt you is never going to be the one who heals you. I wanted him to admit he was wrong. I wanted him to tell me why he did what he did. It's insanity, really, because we want this toxic person to give us closure, but we won't get it from them. **We are trying to make logic out of an illogical situation.** It's just a hard thing to admit that he didn't love me and all those years were a lie. Do you know what it feels like to

> *We are trying to make logic out of an illogical situation.*

know that 33 years of your life were a lie? It's fucking painful. That's why people trying to tell you to forgive, move on, etc., are wrong, even though they probably mean well.

> *"If we cannot forgive and move on, perhaps we need to move on first and forgiveness will follow."*

I read a great quote from Untamed by Glennon Doyle: **"If we cannot forgive and move on, perhaps we need to move on first and forgiveness will follow."** I don't want to forgive, but I know it is a process I must go through. I hope that, as I move on, forgiveness will follow.

I really love this quote. While I do not believe he impacts my life in any way as far as bitterness, I don't know if I've truly forgiven him. I understand why he did it, but that doesn't excuse his behavior. It's definitely a process and a daily choice to check myself and how I am feeling.

Others say that acceptance is the key to recovery. You can recover by accepting it, understanding exactly how it happened, forgiving yourself, and grieving your way through it. As painful as it is, you have to grieve. It's like a death; it truly is. It's a hard reality that you have to walk through. I've been in your shoes. If I can do it, you can, too!

Chapter 11:

Betrayal

February 21st, 2023:

I think I'm in a weird stage of trying to heal from the betrayal because trust was the cornerstone of our marriage. He betrayed my trust. He broke my heart. They lied right to my face.

I often said that trust was the cornerstone of our marriage, and as I'm writing this, I wonder if that was true. Did he say it was so that he could get away with doing things that made him not trustworthy and I wouldn't notice? That's the hard part about looking back on your life with a narcissist. You really don't know what's real and what's not real. You can never ask them because they will not tell you the truth. They've curated lies, and their façade is so real to them. They will also never admit that they've done anything wrong and will often blame you for whatever you bring up. It's madness and futile to try to gain understanding.

I have heard it said that you are not going to find the healing you want from the person that hurt you. You must move forward and heal yourself because there is no kind of healing coming from the hand of your toxic ex.

Keep moving forward! I know you can do it, and I'm rooting for you!

Chapter 12:

Shit List

February 26th 2023:

It's been a few good days. I can actually think about them and not cry. He did me a favor because now I can be happy. I see so many things he wouldn't give me. Basic needs for God sake. I can't wait to see what the future holds. Today I am shopping for a new laptop, tomorrow I am signing off on the house, and will book my trip to Paris. I know this is something I have to do. Something I want to do.

The next day, we were going to sign off on the house, and I was going to book my solo trip to Paris. The trip to Paris was very important as the next step in my healing. He would often ask me if we were going to book our trip, but when I would say yes, he would get mad and say we didn't have the money. He would talk about how he wanted to buy a new car or put solar on the house, but going to Paris was out of the question. This is a tactic of the narcissist. They have the money for the things they want to spend money on, but not for something you may want. Talking about booking the trip is part of future faking and keeps you on the hook. We often see future faking at the beginning of a relationship, but it can happen anytime in a relationship as part of the manipulation.

I just remember that it was a good day. I had had a few good days of being able to think about them together and not being sad or crying. Being removed from my marriage for about six months, I can see that even the basic wants and needs of my life were not being met anymore by him towards the end of our marriage. It breaks my heart to think about the shell of a woman that I was when we got divorced. I remember sitting in the mediator's office and not knowing how to get a divorce, not knowing how to go through the process. It's heartbreaking to think back to who I was. I was very quiet and very still. I didn't want to upset him. I didn't want him to get mad at me. I didn't want to talk because then he wouldn't have anything to get mad at me about. But then he would get mad that I was not participating in conversations or not talking or things like that.

Selling the house at this time after our divorce was hard. I had to navigate that all alone and didn't feel like I had anyone to talk to. I could see that making decisions was still hard for me. When you're in the throes of abuse, you have a hard time making decisions for fear of being wrong. Even months later, I had difficulty making such big decisions on my own. I missed my husband who always helped me make decisions, but I no longer had a husband. It's weird to think about that. I didn't miss my ex, but I missed that partnership. The "good" times would randomly come to memory and make me miss him. I would have to remind myself of the bad times so my brain could heal.

Something I learned along the way was to make a shit list. When my mind wandered to the "good" times, I was recommended to look at a list of all the bad things he did to me. Write it all down! You aren't posting this list or sharing it with anyone. It's just to remind you as to why you left! It is very effective and highly recommended!

In hindsight, I am proud of myself for getting through the tough times alone. There are resources out there in the community to help you. We heal in community and conversation, so find your community. They're there to help you.

Chapter 13:

Boundaries

March 26th, 2023:

I'm sick of crying over you, ex, while you're off not giving two shits about me! Fuck you, you dick! Fuck you both!

I felt like this was a really important journal entry to share because it's real and raw. Not even nine months since our divorce, and he had moved on while I was unraveling 33 years of marriage, lies, betrayal, sadness, and mind games. What was real? What wasn't?

I wanted to include this journal entry because I wanted to showcase how much anger plays a factor in healing. I remember that I went from this point of anger, where you could easily slash their tires, to almost like a righteous anger of wanting to have my voice heard, have my story heard, and help others heal from their pain. The amount of anger I feel towards narcissists and people who are abusive is unbelievable. I just don't understand it. Rationally, I understand how their trauma has caused them to become who they are, but that doesn't excuse their behavior. It just explains it. It's something that's important to remember because I used to be this person who would say, "I know why they do this," and so I would almost give them an excuse to behave a certain way, but it does not excuse their behavior.

While I was healing, well-meaning people talked about how I shouldn't feel anger towards him, but I think it's a very necessary emotion. Mind.org.uk writes that anger is a normal, healthy emotion. There are many different reasons why we might feel angry. We may feel anger at having been treated badly or unfairly by others. Our anger may be a reaction to difficult experiences in our daily lives, our past, or in the world around us. Or it may be a way to cope with other emotions.

Anger alerts you to when something in your life needs to change. We often feel anger when our boundaries are being crossed, even boundaries we do not know we have. Thinking back to how angry I was in our marriage, I understand now it was because I truly believed I was being treated unfairly and my boundaries were being crossed. Mind you, I didn't even know what boundaries were; I just knew that I felt taken advantage of in many situations in my life.

I also heard from others who told me that I shouldn't publicly talk about these things and that I should just heal quietly. It confused me because if no one is talking about this kind of abuse, then other women may sit for 33 years in their marriage like I did. When I started to understand what had happened to me, I remember how ashamed and stupid I felt. People came out of the woodwork to say, "Did you know my first marriage was abusive?" and I responded with, "No, because we don't talk about these kinds of things."

Shame is broken in community and conversation!

We have to continue to talk about abuse so that we can all heal together and hopefully save others from this fate.

> *Shame is broken in community and conversation!*

The ultimate act of self-love for me came when I learned to set boundaries* for myself. I used to think that boundaries were me telling others what to do! As a former people pleaser, it sounded like torture to have to tell others what to do. I now understand that boundaries are the limits and rules we set for ourselves within relationships. People with healthy boundaries can say "no" to others when they want to, but they are also comfortable opening themselves up to intimacy and close relationships.

Boundaries have truly set me free in my toxic relationships.

Chapter 14:

DARVO

4 April 2023:

*As I heal, I think back to all the years of fights.
God, he's been a narcissist all along and I didn't know.
Would I have ever left? No. Not in the state I was in. I
never would have left. I would have stayed forever. We
wouldn't have Evan. I am so sad. Why do I always have
to be the one who heals? God, thank you for giving me
such empathy. Thank you for making me into the
amazing person I am. Continue to heal my broken heart
and lead me down the path to healing.*

As I'm reading through my journal, I see things from years past, and I think to myself, "Man, he's always been a narcissist!" The thing I find in my journal entries is that he's had a pattern of DARVO, a pattern of using therapists against me, a pattern of lying about women, and a pattern about the smear campaign. He's had all the patterns, but I spent so many years trying to convince him to treat me better and that I was worth treating better! I would recycle more, serve in the community with him more, and do what he wanted, like hiking and anything else he was interested in, but I was still treated like what I had done didn't matter. I just wanted to convince him that I was worth loving. He was never going to be convinced. Every once in a while, he would act pleased with me. This is called breadcrumbing.

I used to live my life off of breadcrumbs until, one day, I realized I was starving. Every time we would go back to that "good place" where things seemed headed in the right direction, I would get excited and hang on a little bit longer. It wasn't until the last couple of years of our marriage that I even considered leaving. The good times were getting to be fewer and farther between. I was getting weary. I didn't understand why other people had better marriages than I did. I know comparison can be the "thief of joy," according to Theodore Roosevelt, but I longed for a life where I felt comfortable to be myself. To this day, I enjoy seeing other people enjoying their life in the way they like. I envy that, and instead of it being a bad thing, I see it as a thing I want and will strive to achieve with my next relationship. I will only settle for being my true self from now on. I hope you will, too!

When we go through this world being our true selves, our tribe finds us. The people that truly love us find us. The people that should be in our lives find us.

Chapter 15:

Journaling

10 April 2023:

Today was a good day. I am starting to feel alive again. I cleaned out the linen closet yesterday, made a huge donation to the animal hospital of blankets and towels, created another journal, made a big sale with my business, and signed up for some vendor events with my other business. I'm ready to do something fun with my business. I always come alive when I'm creating. I am so thankful for Peaches - she loves me and keeps me company, my comfy bed, and that I no longer have my ex in my life to make me feel bad about myself. I spent too many years sad and alone. Why couldn't he just love me? Why is he so damaged? Thank you God that you opened my eyes, gave me discernment, gave me a great therapist, and showed me the way out.

I think this is why it's so important to journal. Each day is different, but you can really start to see the fog beginning to clear when you read back on your progress. You have to celebrate the little wins, not just the big wins. When you only focus on the big wins, you may not be able to see your progress.

I remember a day when I had gotten out of bed, and I went to the bathroom mirror and encouraged myself by saying, "Great job getting out of bed today!" It may feel weird at first, but your mind, body, and soul need so much care. You've spent time hearing toxic words spoken to you, that it's time to treat yourself like a houseplant. Drink plenty of water, get some sunshine, and speak kindly to yourself.

The flurry of activity I mentioned in my journal entry is something that you'll see happening, too. As the sun started to shine more and my healing journey moved forward, I was having a good day. I took advantage of the good day to do some projects around my home to make me feel better. It helped me feel like I had some control of my surroundings, and my space felt clear. I am an organizer at heart, but moving after my divorce made me want to clear the clutter even more.

Take advantage of the times you have to move and clear away things that no longer bring you joy in your new life. When my ex and I were dividing things up in our home, I did not take many things with me. I knew that I wanted a fresh start. You may find you will feel the same.

Chapter 16:

Trauma Responses

May 27th, 2023:

I didn't even know myself anymore to know I wanted to leave. I'm learning who I am and what I like. I am connecting to myself and to God in Me.

*T*his was a really important day because I started to get more clarity, and I realized that I didn't even know who I was when I left the marriage. I was a shell of a woman. I didn't know who I was, what I liked, or what I wanted. It broke my heart. He broke my heart and shattered it into a million pieces, and when I walked away from the marriage, I truly thought that I would just walk away from the problem and I was going to feel better. But instead, I've been putting my heart back together, and it's been with God's help. I spent the majority of my marriage asking God to heal my broken heart. It's so sad to think about that. I just wanted my pain to stop. I wanted my heart to not be broken. Someone who loves you doesn't make you feel unloved and like your heart is broken. I'm so unbelievably tired of praying that prayer. I never want to pray that prayer ever again. I never want my heart so broken that that's the only thing I can say.

That's what the narcissist will do to you. They will leave you in a million little pieces and walk away without remorse. I spent 33 years with him and felt thrown away like trash. We may want to speculate that they feel bad or think about you, but they only remember what you did for them and how useful you were to them. It's a painful, harsh reality.

This journal entry was written eight months after our divorce. Each month, I would get even more clarity. I could see that he had torn me down as far as I could go. I wasn't able to make decisions on my own. I was frozen in fear of even deciding if I should stay or if I should go. Nothing felt right.

This is called the fight, flight, freeze, and fawn responses. Simplypsychology.org says these responses are a person's way of coping with stress and threats. The freeze and fawn responses can undermine self-protection. In an abusive relationship, people may use the freeze response to suppress painful feelings or the fawn response to attend to the perpetrator's needs.

- **Fight**: facing any perceived threat aggressively.
- **Flight**: running away from danger.
- **Freeze**: unable to move or act against a threat.
- **Fawn**: immediately acting to try to please to avoid any conflict.

I was stuck in a perpetual state of freeze. I couldn't make even the simplest decisions on my own any longer. Every decision upset him, or he would tell me how wrong I was. Nothing felt good or right. I felt so small that I didn't even know that leaving could be a possibility. This is why many women in abuse end up staying longer than they probably should. There is a freeze state in which many are stuck in because they have been programmed and told they won't survive without their spouse, no one will want them, or they're so dumb that they can't even make the simplest decisions on their own.

Therapy truly helped me to understand that even my needs were important. I used to tell my ex about my dreams of helping spread joy to women, and he would tell me that it was not a realistic dream. He often wanted me to make money, which I did by working as a speech therapist and when I owned my own online boutique, but dreaming about doing something like speaking on stage to other women sounded silly and impractical to him. It's not a surprise that I have now grown a business where I speak to women and encourage them to live their lives their way.

As you heal, you may find that the dreams you pushed down to help keep the peace will start to surface again. Perhaps you're supposed to write a book, take up painting, learn to dance, or start a podcast like I did! Look for the clues. They will appear as you take this magical journey.

Chapter 17:

Manipulation

July 2nd, 2023:

Today, I recorded my episode for my podcast. I started sobbing and felt raw and exposed. I also felt like I did when he would reprimand me. I will be okay, but I am sad and don't know if this is right. This is how women stay in abusive relationships. This is how they stay quiet.

On this day, I recorded episode 1 of my podcast. I put it off for a long time and actually had to record it twice to be more clear and not sound like I was rambling too much. In the end, it doesn't matter how it sounds.

This episode was just me telling my story of who I am, how I met my ex, our marriage, how I left, and my healing journey. When I was done with my episode, I broke down sobbing. I felt so raw and exposed. I truly felt like I did when he would reprimand me when we were married. Anytime I had an opinion on a social issue or something that happened in our family or friend group, I was reprimanded for thinking the way I did. I never felt like I could share my life with him for fear of being scolded like a child. It's funny to think that 18 months later, I now share all of my life stories and anything I want with practically reckless abandon on a global podcast. Now there's no one to stop me!

In my manipulated state, I was careful with my words, even if he wasn't with me. I recently had a friend tell me that she felt like I was much more confident in how I spoke and the type of advice I gave. I know it's because I am no longer manipulated into thinking that somehow, he'll find out what I said and scold me for saying the wrong thing. My conscience used to be my ex, and it even overshadowed the voice of the Holy Spirit.

I could have held a conference on why I liked the color pink, and he would find a way to tell me how embarrassing it was or how ridiculous it was to like pink. Every single thing you like or think is wrong in their eyes, and they will tell you so. I remember a time when I agreed with a group on a social issue, but he hissed at me and made me tell him why I felt that way. It put me on the spot and made me feel bad. It also kept me silent. Narcissists will often make you feel bad or belittle your opinions to keep you quiet.

All of this is by design. It's to keep you manipulated. I feel like this is how women stay in abusive relationships and how they stay quiet. I spent so many years quiet because it was easier and felt safer. I have since realized that it's better for the abuser but not for the victim. Having to stay quiet for so long was the catalyst for me breaking through and finding my voice. I think this is why sharing my story on my podcast was so overwhelming and triggering to me. I no longer feel this way, but that day, the old familiar feelings of manipulation crept in. I could hear his voice telling me that my story was not important. I could hear him saying that no one was going to care about what I had to say. I sat in my office and sobbed, and then I moved on. I let the emotions out, and I let them go.

Good or bad, my episode is there for all to hear and serves as a guiding light for others who may be unaware of the warning signs of abuse, much like my 22-year-old self.

Chapter.18:

Heard

July 19th, 2023:

During therapy yesterday and while talking to Gabi, I said, "Oh my God, I started a podcast because I never felt listened to, heard, or understood." Wow!

This has been a significant revelation in my healing journey! Doing inner child work, figuring out as I'm doing therapy, and as I'm getting clarity, I realized that I haven't been heard or listened to all my life. I've been loud since childhood, my nickname being "Louda" because that's how you pronounce Laura in Spanish. I've always wanted to be heard. I spent a lot of years in my childhood and in my marriage feeling like what I had to say wasn't important. I was told I was too much, and how I'm feeling now is that I will no longer be dimming my light for anyone. No one in this entire world should have to dim their light because someone else is uncomfortable.

This is where setting boundaries will start to be important. When you set boundaries, you learn what's important and not important in your life and how you want to be treated. Once you know how you want to be treated, you can start teaching others around you how to treat you. Being told to be quiet or that my opinion was unimportant was no longer okay with me.

I allowed him to say, "You're too much," and let many people around me say, "You're too much," so I shrunk myself to be smaller. I walked on eggshells so that I could be smaller and quieter. I recently found a note I had saved in my phone. This was about a year and a half before we got divorced. It was titled "Strategies." This was what was on the list for me to try to help salvage our marriage:

- Do minimal talking
- Do not comment on anything he says
- Be agreeable

- Do my talking, commenting, and disagreeing with other people
- See how this works

Is this the saddest list you've ever seen? This is how desperate I was. I was willing to completely change who I was as a person and basically blend into the woodwork so that he wouldn't be upset with me. I love this quote from a friend's t-shirt line: **If I'm a lot, then go find less (Glitch Mob Podcast)**. It really speaks to how I feel.

Nothing is ever good enough with a narcissist. Now, I no longer dim my light to accommodate others. I am no longer quiet. I picked up a microphone on this day, and started talking, and I will continue talking until everyone in this world has heard about narcissistic abuse. *I heal loudly for those women out there who have felt that being quiet was safer.*

> *I heal loudly for those women out there who have felt that being quiet was safer.*

Chapter 19:

Reactive Abuse

July 28th 2023:

More stuff to unpack. Somewhere along the way I made myself look too resilient and friends don't come around. I hate that people I know still follow my ex on social media. It makes me feel like they don't get it, they don't get me. That is the theme running through my life right now. Who gets me? Who understands me? I don't know. No one. That fucking hurts. I'm so confused! God, show me where to go or what to do. I feel like I want to run away. God, heal me, show me who my friends are, who will be there for me. Being alone will help me to sort out who I am away from the noise of the world. It's okay to be alone right now. It is for a reason and a season.

*T*his was really important and it was a start of me understanding secondary gaslighting. People were asking me, "Are you sure that happened to you?" and "Why did you stay so long?" I knew people were continuing to follow him on social media, and because he had curated his new, wonderful life with his "new" girlfriend, it looked like he was happy. It really looks like he got away from the crazy ex-wife, and he's finally happy.

While they may play dumb, they aren't. Narcissists know exactly what they're doing. They turn it on, and they turn it off. Do you know how I know this? They don't abuse everyone in their life? They only abuse whoever is their target. When you are the target of a covert narcissist, it's hard for others to see that anything is wrong. No one else will see the abuse if they are not the target of the abuse. Everyone else thought he was the best thing ever, so I sound like I'm making things up. When I started to talk to other women who had been in a marriage to a covert narcissist, I finally felt seen, heard, and validated! I couldn't believe that someone else knew what I was going through! The most important thing to me was that I didn't feel like others thought I was lying about my experience.

When you've been psychologically abused, you don't have physical bruises on your body. I tell people, "This is what happened to me." Instead of saying, "Let me help you bandage those broken parts," they ask, "Are you sure that happened to you?" If someone who had been punched in the eye by their abuser came to you and said I've been abused, you would not look at them and say, "Are you sure that happened to you?"

Secondary gaslighting has been one of the most surprising things to me. Their façade is curated, and the smear campaign is being carried out behind the scenes. It's all been going on for a long time. The story being told behind your back was that your marriage was difficult, that you were difficult; maybe you're even being told that to your face. If only you would be more agreeable, then you wouldn't be "so difficult and hard to be around." I tried to be agreeable; I tried to do lots of things, but it was never enough. Actually, I wasn't the one who was difficult. I was just being manipulated into thinking that I was.

There were times when I wouldn't even be talking, and one of my kids would start a conversation that sounded like this:

Them: "Mom, you seem upset."

Me: "No, I'm not upset. I'm just sitting here."

Them: "You're using that voice that you use when you're not upset to pretend that you're not upset."

Me: "No, I'm not upset."

This would go on a few times, and then the button is pushed until you finally get upset, and then everyone can say, "See, you're upset." This cycle is called reactive abuse* but I like the other term I heard, which is reactive rage. The way I felt in this situation was full of rage. How do you explain to someone that you are NOT feeling a certain way? It's psychologically abusive.

This is all part of the secondary gaslighting. My children and I have had healing from this. As they remember the incidents, we apologize to each other. We now have open lines of communication to bring up the things that hurt us in the past. This has taken time, effort, and lots of therapy, but it can be done! I encourage you to attempt reconciliation if that is something you want.

They knew the theme running through the family was that "mom is crazy" and "mom is difficult," but they understand the truth now. I thought I was an angry mom, but I understand now that I just didn't feel supported in my marriage and as a mother. I was told I was a bad mom. When I needed help around the house from my spouse because we had a five-year-old, a three-year-old, and a newborn who had special needs, I was told that I should learn how to schedule my day better, and then I would be able to handle everything. I was also reminded that "This is the life you wanted." While he did participate in our household chores to a certain extent, he did not attempt to understand how to support me emotionally.

I don't know how many nights I went to bed crying, laying right next to him crying, and him not caring. He would be dead asleep. They sleep just fine. They don't care. They have things to do, and they don't care. He's abused me all day long. His day is done, and he can sleep soundly.

As I was healing, I noticed how some friends were no longer coming around. I tried to understand, but speaking to good friends, and learning new information in wellness classes, made me understand what was happening. Manchal Kalra wrote about this on Linkedin. Why do we lose friends on our healing and personal growth journey? she asked. "Sometimes, people might distance themselves from you because they feel uncomfortable with the changes you're making.

Maybe they're used to the old you and don't know how to relate to the new and improved you. Or, maybe, they feel like they're being judged for not making similar changes in their own lives.

It's also possible that your healing journey brings up some uncomfortable feelings for those around you because you choose to stay rooted in your authenticity and speak your truth.

Maybe they've been through similar struggles but haven't yet found the courage to confront them."

As hard as it is, and believe me, I know it is, you must continue to choose yourself and your healing journey over chasing friends who no longer want to be in your life. It's normal to grieve the loss of those who have chosen to leave your life. Losing friends will only make room for new friends you haven't yet met!

The people who are supposed to be there will still be there. I'm grateful for the friends who have chosen to stay in my life, and I treasure them even more.

Chapter 20:

Get Curious

September 7th, 2023:

I'm tired of being strong. I want to be okay, but as their wedding gets closer, all I can do is be sad about the fact that he discarded me for someone else, like that lying dog that he is. I am so not fully healed yet, and he is off marrying someone else! Fuck it hurts! God help me heal. I am too sad!

*W*hew, I can feel the pain in my journaling here. No amount of therapy can prepare you for the pain, rejection, and heartbreak you will feel when the person you thought you were going to spend your life with, the father of your children, the person you gave your heart to, the person you trusted the most in this world betrays you in such a cold and dirty way. Nothing could have prepared me for how I would feel.

After 33 years, he was marrying someone else. We hadn't even been divorced for a year. I have thought about this, and it truly wasn't just that he was marrying someone else, but that he was marrying *her*. That it was her compounded my pain.

He promised me that she was just a friend.

He promised me that nothing was going on.

He promised me that I could trust him.

Let this serve as a warning or wake-up call. You are not crazy, and they are never *just* friends. If your gut is telling you something is wrong, get curious. I know how that sounds, since looking back, I never would have questioned him, because he would get so mad if I did, but healed Laura knows better! That's manipulation! If they make a bigger deal about *how* you're asking a question rather than answering it, that's manipulation.

Looking back with my healed vision, I would have questioned him and maybe even confronted the other woman if they had flirted in front of me. That's easy to say now, being on the other side. But I know I wouldn't have wanted to rock the boat then. I was definitely too scared.

We get suspicious for a reason. It's good to be curious. I remember my therapist telling me that in therapy. Be curious about why he feels a certain way so you can understand why he is saying what he is saying or why he wants certain things. It helps us to unpack things.

We should be curious about our own wants and needs as well. This "being curious" has truly helped in my relationships as I've moved forward. Asking someone, "Can you help me understand what you mean by that?" has been beneficial in my healthy relationships. When you ask that question, you can see who is healthy and who is not because toxic people will take offense to being asked questions. They feel attacked. Keep using your healthy relationship skills, and let the toxic people fall out of your life.

Unfortunately, when you're dealing with a narcissist, you're weeding through lies, but my point still stands. Get curious. Ask questions. Someone who wants a better relationship with you will not be offended by what you ask. They will try and explain and work on bettering your relationship. They will not tell you that you're crazy or rude for even asking the question. Others who say you are the problem for questioning them, being curious, or generally just wanting to understand what is going on are not healthy, may be manipulating you, and may only want it their way or the highway.

As you learn what's important in your life, you'll want to learn healthy ways to interact with friends, family, and new relationships. When you get to the point that you are happy and at peace being on your own, you'll be more particular about who you let into your inner circle.

I started to see my circle of friends and family like a bullseye. The friends closest to the middle are my friends who are the closest to me and my heart. They are the ones that know my heart and want to hear my stories. The further out in the bullseye, the more casual the relationship. Not everyone should have access to your heart. Your circle of friends may get smaller and smaller, but the quality will go up. It's important to remember that.

As you start to treat yourself with tender loving care and taking care of your heart, you will see that you deserve the best for your life. You won't tolerate garbage from anyone anymore. You deserve the best for the rest of your life.

Chapter 21:

Rewrite The Story

Sept 12th 2023:

Just had a great session with my holistic therapist and just now listened to "My Love", our wedding song. I cried but it did not affect me like I thought it would. Yay! Next is our wedding pictures. Okay, wedding pictures didn't bother me. It's okay if they would have, but they don't. I just hate his face so much for replacing me.

As my ex's wedding date to his "new" girlfriend got closer, I was understandably feeling sad, confused, replaced, and discarded. My heart was still hurting. While many people helped me feel like I was not discarded but rather set free from the terrible life I was living, it still hurt. I still think back to the way I felt when he would flirt with her in front of me, and I can still feel my stomach tying up in knots.

As I healed, I decided to try different types of healing. While I love and continue with my private therapist, I wanted to try different holistic approaches. I did meditation, hypnosis, tapping, and prayer. During this holistic session, I learned about what was triggering me and learned how to move through it. During this particular holistic session, she used my ex's upcoming wedding to help me release another level of sadness by looking at my wedding pictures and listening to my wedding song. I cried and got the pain out, and even now, looking at the pictures, they don't bother me. I understood through my healing that these feelings are all normal and that I shouldn't hold them inside. I needed to let them out. It's also important to note that having these feelings, even almost a year later, is normal and ok! You have a soft heart and have had a lot of love for a lot of years. You don't turn that off like a faucet, despite what your ex may be doing or saying.

"Go and laugh in the places that you had previously cried. Rewrite the story."

I read this quote that I really like: **"Go and laugh in the places that you had previously cried. Rewrite the story."** Listening to our wedding song and looking at our wedding pictures reminded me of a better time, but also of the chaos that was to come, and all the tears I had shed for him. It's important to go and laugh in those places! Don't avoid them! Rewrite the story!

It felt good to do an activity like this and to see my progress. Not even a year after our divorce, I was thriving in my healing, and he was getting remarried.

I want to take this time to remind you about the narcissist and his need for supply. He must always have someone so that the shame does not bubble to the surface and make him look at himself. You must constantly remind yourself that this is not about you. Even if they spew hateful words at you and tell you that it *is* your fault, you do not have to believe them. They will replace you at any time. They will find someone who will not call them out on their crap. They will find someone who "follows the rules." It's not worth living in misery to stay in a relationship with a toxic person like this.

Thinking about him getting remarried made me sad, but I had more joy in my life than I probably had my entire life! I spent my life in misery in our marriage, and the pain I felt from his betrayal was terrible, but this life I was living in freedom and joy was worth every tear that I have shed.

While it's not easy to just move on, remind yourself of all the good you have had away from your ex. Look at the strength you've had to go it alone! Look at the joy you've had away from him! Look at the healing of your mind, body, and spirit, all because you chose yourself!

Choosing yourself is never selfish, especially when you've been living life in chaos and pain. Now is the time to keep choosing you and your healing! A new adventure awaits you, and you have to be strong to go on that adventure!

As always, I know you can do it, and I'm rooting for you!

Chapter 22:

Lack of Empathy

October 10th 2023:

I gasped audibly when I saw the Eiffel Tower. I couldn't believe it! I cried when I stopped to take pictures. I am so proud of myself for doing this alone, but I am ready to be back home and find someone to spend life with. I thought I had him, but he chose a different route. Life's too short to be unhappy and miserable. I am glad I got divorced but it still sucks.

*G*oing to Paris was a dream I had always had. In 2020 we were going to be celebrating our 30th anniversary. We talked about going to Paris to celebrate and renew our vows under the Eiffel Tower. Even now, it's still a dream I have. It sounds so romantic. Maybe I'm just being a silly American, but it truly sounds magical to me.

The year before, my mother had been fighting and recovering from cancer. It was hard to make plans, though he often asked me if I truly wanted to go to Paris because I wouldn't actually buy tickets to go. The lack of empathy is evident. "Do you even want to go?", he would ask. He could never look at the situation of my mother nearly dying as a reason not to want to leave the country. I just must be indecisive and not *really* want to go to Paris. My priority at that time was my mother. We weren't sure if we would lose her or not, and eventually we did. At the beginning of the pandemic, we lost her, and instead of planning a trip to Paris, I planned a funeral with my siblings. It was a terrible time of grieving, as you can imagine.

With a lack of empathy as one of their characteristics, narcissists are often too self-absorbed to care about how others are feeling. I truly feel like this was the beginning of the end of our marriage. Soon after my mother's funeral, the world shut down because of the pandemic. Planning a trip to Paris was not to be, not only because the world was shut down but because I was also grieving the loss of my mother. As time went on, I decided to retire from my career as a speech therapist and began an online boutique to make some extra money. Thinking back to that time, I was unbelievably overwhelmed with sadness because of the pandemic, but also because my mother was gone.

In 2021, we had another devastating loss when we lost our sister-in-law to the worldwide virus. I was barely able to stay afloat from the grief in my life and then was hit with this terrible tragedy. My ex would come home from work and wonder why I hadn't been working, asking me why I was still sad. I remember trying so hard to get out of my sadness because I thought he was right. I thought I shouldn't be sad anymore. It was too many months of still being sad, according to him. I started to believe it as well. I had never grieved the loss of two family members, and maybe I should be "over it" by now. PS: I'm still not over it.

My kids and I laugh about this now because it's such a ridiculous statement, but he used to say, "I just choose to be happy." While that seems like a good thing to say, it's very flippant to people who are genuinely struggling with sadness and depression from grief. My feelings were valid, but he didn't know how to be empathetic about it. They have empathy; they just choose when to use it and when not to. Like I said, this felt like the ending stages of our marriage, and so he really didn't care how I was feeling. He just wanted to know why I wasn't working. Money was definitely an important thing to him, and my taking time to grieve didn't make sense to him.

When we divorced, I knew I wanted to go to Paris for a symbolic healing trip. I wanted to see the Eiffel Tower in person, I wanted to see it sparkle at night, see it from the Trocadero, and I wanted to eat croissants in a cafe. I got to do all of those things!

I went with a tour group, and they knew why I was there. Two of the ladies in the group had left their husbands after 38 years and 41 years, respectively. They told me it was never too late for my "happily ever after." You never know where you're going to find cheerleaders. I found two in Europe!

When we got into Paris, and I saw the Eiffel Tower in the distance I audibly gasped! The entire tour bus turned around and practically yelled, "What?" because I had scared them with my gasp. I said, "You guys, it's the Eiffel Tower!" They all laughed. They knew why I was so excited. They knew why I was there.

Many of them looked at me, smiled, and said, **"You did it, Laura. You did it!"** I truly did do it! It was a symbolic thing I needed to do to heal. By the end of the trip, I could feel my life changing. I felt ready to move forward. I felt ready to make big changes in my life.

> *"You did it, Laura. You did it!"*

- Dating? Perhaps.
- Writing a book about my life experience? Definitely. (Thanks for reading it, by the way.)
- Warning other women of the narcissist's lies and tactics on my global podcast? Yes, and Amen.

I have chosen not to stay quiet like I had for 55 years of my life. I spent my life trying to be myself and being told I was too much. I will never again dim my light to make other people feel better about themselves or to make them feel more comfortable in my presence. You shouldn't either! I believe too many of us are walking through this world alive but not truly living.

Bronnie Ware reported that the most common regret said by the dying was: "I wish I had the courage to live a life true to myself, not the life others expected of me."

Don't go to your death bed being miserable and sad, only to say you were married for 50 years. Are you truly happy? Are you being respected? Are you being celebrated and not just tolerated? You deserve to live a life where you are truly happy. You deserve the best in life.

Like my travel-mates told me, "It's never too late for your happily ever after."

Epilogue

At the writing of this book, I am doing really well. I continue with my healing practices of therapy, prayer, journaling, and holistic therapies to continue to heal my mind, body, soul, and heart. We didn't get here overnight, and we won't be healed overnight.

But there is hope! Here are a few updates about me and my life.

I no longer have pain thinking about the past or even thinking about him. Occasionally, I will have a bad dream, but it's often because something has come up about my ex, and my subconscious tries to deal with it. When I am triggered like this, I use tools to help me move through it and set boundaries with myself and anyone else that may need it in regard to my ex. Here are some ways to unpack your triggers that I learned in my Me Season* group:

- Ask: What about this is giving me this reaction?
  o Why?
- When have I felt this way before?
- What am I telling myself at this moment? "The story I'm telling myself is…"
- What can I do right now to get back to center?
- What can I do next?
  o Get your emotions out of your body.

I now have a top 10% global podcast called That's Where I'm At Podcast, where I talk to women just like myself who have been through psychological or physical abuse. I use my platform to spread awareness and empowerment. I hope to take my "show on the road" and speak to women in person on stages, sharing my experience and giving them hope about life after abuse. You will also find me as a guest on other podcasts, spreading awareness and sharing all of the tricks and tactics narcissists use so that you won't fall into the same trap I did for 33 years!

I continue to create funny videos to make you laugh and educate you on red flags and ways to heal after abuse. It's ironic that making funny videos about my divorce would turn into a business!

I spent many years not dreaming, being told my dreams were impractical or frivolous because I couldn't make money from them. I know now that nothing can stop you when you have a dream in your heart. I am a serial entrepreneur at heart, and I now dream with reckless abandon. I am not scared to try and fail. To me, it's the staying down that makes you a failure. I often say, **"Fall down seven, get up eight."**

> *"Fall down seven, get up eight."*

Divorce is hard, and sometimes you might feel like you should always have good thoughts about your ex. Well, I'm here to give you permission to sometimes walk in your angry and mad feelings. As a reminder, don't go to jail for anyone: no property damage and no bodily harm.

Here are some honest things I did that I don't feel bad about doing:

- Ripping a large family picture in half, making sure I ripped it right between my face and his
- Not intervening when my grown children chose not to have a relationship with their father

- Telling the truth on my own podcast and as a guest on other podcasts
- Not forgiving him for a long time
- Not wishing him well
- Not giving him access to any family photos that I had stored in my cloud
- Using the word fuck many times while unraveling my 33 years with him, even though I was told I shouldn't cuss

You now have permission to do that thing you've been wanting to do. Burn your marriage license, rip pictures of him in half, and any other thing you can think of.

Don't miss it. Don't miss your life. Straighten your crown and turn your pain into purpose. Instead of focusing on what you feel you will be lacking, embrace what's possible for your future!

I know you can do it...and I'm always rooting for you!

I know you can do it...and I'm always rooting for you!

Boundaries

Each person must decide where they draw the line between preserving their privacy, at least from those with whom they are not intimate, and letting others in. To maintain those lines, they erect boundaries and work to preserve them. Some individuals are more vigilant, and even aggressive, about their firewalls, which can lead to discomfort, if not conflict, with others. But in general, setting healthy boundaries can be a way of preserving one's mental health and well-being.

Breadcrumbing

Breadcrumbing is a manipulative tactic in which someone gives inconsistent or limited communication to another person to keep them interested without fully committing to a relationship. It's also known as hansel and grettelling.

Coping skills

The methods a person uses to deal with stressful situations. These may help a person face a situation, take action, and be flexible and persistent in solving problems.

Codependency

A psychological condition or a relationship in which a person manifesting low self-esteem and a strong desire for approval has an unhealthy attachment to another often controlling or manipulative person (such as a person with an addiction to alcohol or drugs)

Codependent

Sufferers become excessively dependent on other people's needs, particularly when those others are involved in a self-destructive addiction. In their desperation to save these people—to control their thoughts, actions and feelings—

codependents may become as hooked on the addicts as the addicts are hooked on drugs and alcohol.

Cognitive Dissonance

Medical news today defines cognitive dissonance as the discomfort a person feels when their behavior does not align with their values or beliefs. Cognitive dissonance is a psychological phenomenon that occurs when a person holds two contradictory beliefs at the same time.

Covert Narcissist

A covert narcissist is a person with narcissistic personality disorder (npd) who doesn't display the same sense of self-importance as other narcissists. Covert narcissism is also known as "closet narcissism" or "introverted narcissism". Covert narcissism is one of two types of narcissistic personality disorder that is characterized by hypersensitivity and defensiveness. People with covert narcissism are self-conscious, socially insecure, and introverted, which means their narcissistic actions are usually more subtle.

Darvo

Deny, attack, and reverse victim and offender (darvo) is a tactic a person may use to deflect responsibility onto an individual they have abused. It is a form of manipulation a person may use to discredit a survivor's experience.

Delayed Realization

The realization that you are in a narcissistic relationship can be a slow process that involves a range of emotions, including: disbelief, questioning, confusion, bewilderment, intense emotions, fear, sickness, coldness, and worthlessness.

Future Faking

Future faking is a manipulation tactic employed when a narcissist or toxic person promises to fulfill your desires in the future to get something they want in the present — which is often simply to get off scot-free, delay a commitment, obtain resources, or avoid a conflict. Https://katiecouric.com/

Gray Rock Method

The gray rock method is a technique used to make interactions with toxic people as uninteresting and unrewarding as possible. The goal is to make the person lose interest and stop bothering you. The phrase "gray rock" is a metaphor for deflecting or defusing abuse from a partner, family member, or coworker.

Me Season Group

Small group 6-month program with a 1:1 option for the next 6 months put on by coach Gabi Garland of Resilient Heart Podcast

Reactive Abuse

When a victim has been in an abusive relationship for a while, they begin to defend themselves against emotionally violent attacks. The term reactive abuse refers to a victim's defensive response to narcissistic abuse behaviors they have been experiencing over time. In fact, although it is called reactive abuse, the mend project prefers the term reactive defense because a victim is not an abuser. Reactive abuse occurs when the victim becomes the aggressor against the abuser, such as by pushing, punching, kicking, hair pulling, raging, or angry outbursts of aggressive verbal attacks. Reactive abuse is self-defense, not abuse.

Reverse Discard

A reverse discard is a manipulative tactic used by a narcissist to regain control over a former partner. It's when a narcissist intentionally pushes their partner away so that the partner is the one to end the relationship. The narcissist may do this to avoid taking responsibility for their actions or because they're afraid to break up with their partner face-to-face.

Secondary Gaslighting

When you try to talk to your family or friends about what has occurred in the abuse, and they deny that it could have been that way.

Self-Preservation Mode

The meaning of self preservation in a relationship indicates that someone is trying to not lose any part of themselves in a relationship. While this is okay in some ways, it could alienate your partner and make your relationship fail if you are self-preserving too much.

Silent Treatment

Stopping communication to manipulate

Stonewalling

Intentionally ignoring or withdrawing from a conversation

Trauma Bond

Trauma bonding, the bond someone feels towards their partner who is perpetrating abuse, is often the result of these roller-coaster emotions in a relationship. People can't control this attachment. Our brains are wired through our fight or flight response to get through traumatic experiences (like an incident of abuse) by seeking comfort and sometimes, yes, that is from the very person who has harmed us. (shalvacares.org)

Walking On Eggshells

According to collinsdictionary.com: to be very careful about what you say or do to someone because they are easily upset or offended

Check Out More Resources From Laura Richards

- There Is Hope: 52 Keys To Healing After Divorce
- Colorful Reflections: Relaxing Quotes to Inspire Your Day Coloring Book
- Gratitude Journal Notebook Inspirational Paris Eiffel Tower
- The Gratitude Journal For Divorced Women
- God is within her, She will not fall Psalm 46:5 Journal
- Watercolor Paris Travel Journal Notebook Diary 8.5 x 11 Floral Lined Pages
- Zero F*cks Given Journal Fox

Available on Amazon and on
thatswhereimatpodcast.com

Connect with Laura

About the Author

Laura Richards was born in Uruguay, and immigrated to the US when she was three years old. She grew up in Las Vegas, NV with her parents and two siblings. She graduated from high school, then moved to Arizona for college at Northern Arizona University where she received a degree in Secondary Education. She met her ex-husband in college and they raised 3 children together in Las Vegas. Because their third child has special needs, Laura went back to school and got a degree in Speech-Language Pathology. She spent 15 years working for the school district before leaving the profession in 2020.

In 2022, Laura and her ex got a divorce, and Laura started dreaming about her future as a single woman. In the process of healing from her divorce, she began podcasting with sister. Eventually Laura started her own podcast, That's Where I'm At Podcast, after finding out about her ex-husband's betrayal and years of lies. The podcast was inspired by her own need to have a safe place to tell her story of abuse, and give hope and healing to others.

She is also a best-selling author and speaker, speaking to women around the world about narcissistic abuse recovery, how to heal after abuse, and loving yourself through the process!

Printed in Great Britain
by Amazon